# contents

# essentials of good freezing

In comparison with food preserved by other methods, food that is frozen tastes fresher and retains more of its original colour, texture, flavour and nutritional value. And how better to keep produce that is available from the garden or greengrocer in abundance one season but gone the next?

## containers

☐ Freezer containers must be airtight and vapour- and moisture-proof. Glass or ceramic dishes, and metal or foil pans, that can travel from freezer to oven should be encased in a freezer bag or wrapped in heavy foil before storage.

Suitable for freezing: plastic, glass and foil

Storing bagged fish in a shallow container

Freezer bags and plastic wrap: ready to use

☐ Shallow containers of suitable materials are best – allowing for storage in thin layers – because food freezes and thaws more quickly.

☐ Strong plastic containers can be re-used until the seal no longer fits tightly or they crack. Rectangular-shaped containers make best use of freezer space. Plastic takeaway or ice-cream containers are fine to use for freezing but we recommend against putting them in the microwave oven, even for defrosting. If transporting food directly from freezer to microwave oven, we suggest using only cooking containers deemed microwave-safe or specially made freezer-to-microwave disposable plastic containers.

☐ Cleaned and dried cardboard milk, cream, etc, cartons, opened at the top, are good for easy storage of juices, stocks, pasta sauces, soups and other "pourable" foods. Use 300ml, 600ml or 1 litre containers, and seal well after filling. Not only will you know the exact amount you have but also, once the content is frozen solid, the cartons can be stacked on their sides or remain upright – whatever suits the freezer space available.

☐ Freezer bags should be used only once because previous usage may have weakened the material. Care must also be exercised before placing food-filled bags in microwave oven – for thawing, the oven temperature must be set on DEFROST and the bag partially opened or pierced. Follow the instructions on the freezer-bag manufacturer's box, and do not use ordinary plastic bags of any kind in your microwave oven. We do not recommend reheating food in any plastic bags (other than those manufactured for that purpose) in the microwave oven.

Store pasta sauce in an empty milk carton

## packing food

☐ Label and date food before freezing so that you can rotate stock efficiently.

☐ Consider keeping a freezer logbook, to prevent the need to rifle through freezer contents to see what's stored.

☐ When storing in freezer bags, ensure that as much air as possible is worked out of the bag before storing.

☐ Leave empty space at the top of containers or plastic bags containing liquid or semi-solid foods because they expand as they freeze. Usually 2cm to 5cm headspace is recommended.

☐ For faster freezing, do not pack food closely together but spread it out in the freezer until frozen through; it can then be packed more tightly. A full freezer costs less to run than a half-empty one.

☐ For faster freezing and thawing, package food in quantities that suit your lifestyle: smaller quantities for singles and couples, larger ones for families. This way you will also find that you don't defrost more than you need.

☐ Cool all cooked food in the refrigerator, covered, before packaging it for the freezer. Even food that's slightly warm will raise the temperature of other frozen items and could cause deterioration.

☐ For best results, food should be stored at a constant -18°C. Opening the freezer door raises the temperature inside the cabinet, so avoid an overactive elbow. Occasionally check inside your freezer with a thermometer to ensure it is operating at a low enough temperature.

## blanching vegetables

☐ Before freezing any vegetables, blanch by plunging them in a large saucepan or boiler of boiling water (depending on the quantity). As soon as water returns to boil, drain vegetables in colander then plunge them into a large bowl of iced water to quickly reduce the temperature. Drain then pack, in portions, in plastic containers or in freezer bags with as much air removed as possible.

Dating and labelling food prior to placing in freezer

Working air out of freezer bag

Packaging blanched vegetables

# timetable for freezing

These times are a guide only. Frozen foods do not become unsafe to eat even when held for years at -18°C. However, if stored longer than the recommended period, the food's sensory and nutritional properties are diminished.

| Food | Storage life in months -18°C |
|---|---|
| **MEAT** | |
| **Beef,** raw | 18 |
| Mince | 4 |
| Sausages | 4 |
| Cooked casseroles | 3 |
| **Lamb,** raw | 18 |
| Mince | 4 |
| Sausages | 4 |
| Cooked casseroles | 3 |
| **Pork,** raw | 10 |
| Cooked chops | 4 |
| Cooked casseroles | 1 |
| **POULTRY** | |
| **Chicken,** raw | 18 |
| Cooked pieces | 4 |
| Cooked nuggets | 4 |
| Cooked casseroles | 6 |
| **Turkey,** raw | 18 |
| Cooked pieces | 4 |
| **SEAFOOD** | |
| Fatty fish (tuna, salmon, etc), raw | 5 |
| Lean fish (whiting, snapper, etc), raw | 9 |
| Cooked fish dishes | 3 |
| Prawns, cooked and shelled | 5 |
| **FRUIT AND VEGETABLES** | |
| Berries, raw | 24 |
| Stone fruit, raw | 18 |
| Asparagus, blanched | 12 |
| Green beans, blanched | 15 |
| Brussels sprouts, blanched | 15 |
| Carrots, blanched | 18 |
| Corn cobs | 10 |
| Herbs, fresh | 6 |
| **BAKED GOODS** | |
| Sponge cakes | 6 |
| Butter cakes | 4 |
| Cheesecakes | 4 |
| Fruitcakes | 12 |
| Nut and fruit loaves | 4 |
| Biscuits | 8 |
| Muffins | 12 |
| Pancakes and waffles | 2 |

## freezer burn

☐ Freezer burn, and the resultant colour and textural changes in frozen foods, indicates only that the food has not been packed properly or has been frozen incorrectly. The food is still safe to eat but will no longer be either the best-tasting or the best quality. You'll recognise freezer burn when the surface of the food appears dry, with greyish spots, indicating a loss of moisture. Avoid it by making sure packaging is airtight.

☐ Colour changes also occur when foods have been stored too long. Vegetables, for example, become dull and lifeless in appearance, as well as watery and limp.

Freezer burn changes the colour of food

## thawing

☐ Thawing in the refrigerator is the safest of all methods. At least 24 hours is usually required to thaw reasonable-sized portions of foods, such as whole chickens or roasts. Food thawed in the refrigerator may be held for up to 48 hours, if necessary, before being cooked.

☐ Thawing in the microwave oven is the fastest and easiest method. Manufacturers recommend approximate defrosting times for their individual products and state that the oven temperature must always be set on DEFROST.

### refreezing

□ Refreezing is only safe if thawing is not complete, ie, if ice is still present on the food. The food will suffer both loss of quality and flavour, plus refrozen food cannot be kept as long as that which is freshly frozen. It is far safer to cook all thawed foods first before refreezing.

□ Frozen cooked casseroles or dishes that have been thawed should not be frozen a second time.

### unsuitable to freeze

□ Eggs cannot be frozen in the shell; dishes containing cooked egg whites will toughen when frozen.

□ Sauces made with dairy products, like yogurt or cream, have a tendency to separate when thawed.

□ Jellies, unbaked cheesecakes and other dishes made with gelatine become rubbery and assume an altogether different, unflattering texture.

□ Stuffed poultry and all stuffed/rolled/filled/seasoned meats, because the stuffing freezes very slowly creating a high risk of food poisoning.

□ Salad vegetables or any fruit that's to be eaten raw in a salad or dessert, such as any kind of leafy green, pear, cucumber, etc. When frozen then thawed, they break down to become watery and limp. Tomatoes also undergo unpleasant textural changes but can still be frozen and used for cooking.

□ Unbaked yeast dough because freezing destroys yeast in unbaked bread dough, pizza bases, etc. Cook first and then freeze.

### tips

□ Freeze lemon, lime and passionfruit juice in ice-cube containers then re-package in freezer bags for use throughout the year.

□ Store offensive-smelling rubbish, like prawn shells and meat trimmings, in the freezer until garbage collection day.

□ Leftover stock, from a tetra-pack or homemade, can be frozen in ice-cube trays then transferred to freezer bags for storage. Drop one or two as required into sauces, rice dishes, soups, etc, for extra flavour.

Freezing stock in ice-cube form

□ Store raw meat in meal-sized portions, in single layers, rather than in bulk; it both freezes and thaws more quickly.

Storing raw meat in a meal-sized portion

□ Freeze skewered food in freezer bags tied with elastic or string, with the pointed ends of skewers poking out the top so they don't pierce the plastic.

□ Coconut milk or cream can be frozen in ice-cube trays then removed and stored in freezer bags.

□ Keep staples on hand. Milk, bread, butter and cream can all be frozen. Cut and store butter in portions.

□ Freeze oil-based sauces and dressings, such as homemade pesto or crushed anchovies and garlic for caesar salad dressing, in large amounts; because of the oil, they don't freeze solid but keep well so that you can remove whatever amount you require with a hot water-warmed spoon.

Placing chillies in freezer bag

Blended frozen watermelon pieces make a popular treat for kids

☐ Overripe bananas can be frozen whole and used in smoothies, cakes or muffins.

☐ Fresh bananas, frozen on paddle-pop sticks, make great treats for kids.

☐ Peeled and frozen oranges are great for school lunches, as are small bunches of grapes.

☐ To create a treat for kids or adults on a hot summer day, blend frozen watermelon pieces just before serving.

☐ Blend crushed ice with mango for a delicious summer drink; yogurt and mint can be added, too, for another taste sensation.

☐ Mint leaves and thin slices of lime frozen in ice-cube trays make an attractive and gently refreshing addition to a pitcher of iced tea or sparkling water.

☐ Leftover cooked rice and cooked dried (not fresh) pasta freeze very well. Freeze in portions in freezer bags and thaw on DEFROST in the microwave oven.

☐ For quick access during the week, chop and fry about 8 onions and 8 cloves of garlic in olive oil; divide among four small plastic bags. They don't freeze solid so you can just drop the contents of one in your frying pan then take it from there.

☐ Uncooked egg yolks and whites, either beaten lightly together or separated, will store for up to 9 months. However, egg yolks become thick and gluggy, giving disappointing results when cooked. To overcome this, beat the egg yolks lightly with salt or sugar (1 teaspoon of salt or 1 tablespoon of sugar to every 6 egg yolks); freeze in small amounts (the equivalent of one or two eggs); use the salted yolks in savoury dishes and sugared yolks in cakes and desserts.

☐ Freeze fresh herbs, chillies, lemon grass and ginger either dry in freezer bags or finely chopped in ice-cube trays, barely covered with water. Wash and dry the herbs well first; peel and chop the lemon grass; and peel the ginger but freeze in pieces – it grates more easily when frozen. Transfer the frozen cubes to freezer bags for storage.

Cooked rice and pasta – ready to be frozen

## Making your own stock

These recipes can be made up to 4 days ahead and stored, covered, in the refrigerator. Be sure to remove any fat from the surface after the cooled stock has been refrigerated overnight. If the stock is to be kept longer, it is best to freeze it in smaller quantities. *All stock recipes make about 2.5 litres (10 cups).*

### BEEF STOCK

**2kg meaty beef bones**
**2 medium onions (300g)**
**2 sticks celery, chopped**
**2 medium carrots (250g), chopped**
**3 bay leaves**
**2 teaspoons black peppercorns**
**5 litres water (20 cups)**
**3 litres water (12 cups), extra**

Place bones and unpeeled chopped onions in baking dish. Bake in hot oven about 1 hour or until bones and onions are well browned. Transfer bones and onions to large pan, add celery, carrot, bay leaves, peppercorns and water; simmer, uncovered, 3 hours. Add extra water, simmer, uncovered, further 1 hour; strain.

### CHICKEN STOCK

**2kg chicken bones**
**2 medium onions (300g), chopped**
**2 sticks celery, chopped**
**2 medium carrots (250g), chopped**
**3 bay leaves**
**2 teaspoons black peppercorns**
**5 litres water (20 cups)**

Combine ingredients in large pan, simmer, uncovered, 2 hours; strain.

### FISH STOCK

**1.5kg fishbones**
**3 litres water (12 cups)**
**1 medium onion (300g), chopped**
**2 sticks celery, chopped**
**2 medium carrots (250g), chopped**
**3 bay leaves**
**1 teaspoons black peppercorns**

Combine ingredients in large pan, simmer, uncovered, 20 minutes; strain.

### VEGETABLE STOCK

**2 large carrots (360g), chopped**
**2 large parsnips (360g), chopped**
**4 medium onions (600g), chopped**
**12 sticks celery, chopped**
**4 bay leaves**
**2 teaspoons black peppercorns**
**6 litres water (24 cups)**

Combine ingredients in large pan, simmer, uncovered, 1$^1$/2 hours; strain.

Stock is also available in cans or tetra packs. Stock cubes or powder can be used. As a guide, 1 teaspoon of stock powder or 1 small crumbled stock cube mixed with 1 cup water (250ml) will give a fairly strong stock. Be aware of the salt and fat content of stock cubes and powders and prepared stocks.

# poultry

Pies, curries and those other favourites calling for chicken may take a bit more time to prepare than a stir-fry, but variety is, after all, the spice of life.

# chicken and corn pie

*If you only want to serve a single pie at a time, freeze one uncooked then, when you want the second, bake it while it's still frozen.*

**1 large leek (500g),
    sliced thinly**
**2 cloves garlic, crushed**
**750g chicken mince**
**150g fresh baby corn,
    sliced diagonally**
**1 cup frozen peas (160g)**
**60g butter**
**1/4 cup plain flour (35g)**
**2 cups milk (500ml)**
**1 chicken stock cube**
**1/4 cup grated parmesan
    cheese (20g)**
**1/4 cup finely chopped fresh
    flat-leaf parsley**
**310g can creamed corn**
**cooking-oil spray**
**6 sheets ready-rolled puff pastry**
**1 egg, beaten lightly**

1   Heat oil in large heavy-base saucepan; cook leek and garlic, stirring, until leek is soft. Add chicken; cook, stirring, until changed in colour. Stir in baby corn and peas.

2   Melt butter in medium saucepan, add flour; cook, stirring, until mixture thickens and bubbles. Gradually stir in combined milk and crumbled stock cube; stir until sauce boils and thickens. Remove from heat; stir in cheese, parsley and creamed corn. Stir into chicken mixture; cool.

3   Spray two 23cm shallow pie dishes lightly with cooking-oil spray. Preheat oven to hot.

4   Cut 2 pastry sheets in half; attach 2 halves to each of 2 remaining whole sheets on adjacent sides, seal joins together with palette knife. Ease each of these large sheets into each of the prepared dishes gently; trim around edge.

5   Divide cooled chicken mixture between pastry cases. Brush edges with egg; place one of each of the remaining pastry sheets over each pie, trim then press around edge with fork to seal. Brush top of each pie with egg. *[Can be frozen, covered separately, at this stage.]*

6   Bake pies, covered, in hot oven 25 minutes; uncover, bake 20 minutes or until pastry is browned.

SERVES 8

**per serve**  45.8g fat; 3338kJ
**serving suggestion**  Serve with a mixed green salad dressed with balsamic vinegar and extra virgin olive oil.

**tip**  If you want to use fresh peas in this recipe, you need to buy 450g of unshelled fresh peas.

*Joining pastry halves to whole sheets*

*Using fork tines to seal pastry edge*

# chicken broth with ginger dumplings

*Freeze uncooked dumplings and stock separately; frozen dumplings can then be cooked in simmering stock.*

**1 tablespoon peanut oil**
**2 large brown onions (400g),**
  **chopped coarsely**
**2 trimmed celery sticks (150g),**
  **chopped coarsely**
**2 medium carrots (240g),**
  **chopped coarsely**
**1.5kg chicken bones**
**6 kaffir lime leaves, torn**
**2.5 litres water (10 cups)**
**1 small brown onion (80g),**
  **chopped finely**
**2 tablespoons grated fresh ginger**
**2 cloves garlic, crushed**
**750g chicken mince**
**3 green onions, chopped finely**
**3 green onions, sliced**
  **thinly, extra**
**1 cup bean sprouts (80g)**
**2 tablespoons soy sauce**

1  Heat half of the oil in large heavy-base saucepan; cook coarsely chopped brown onion, stirring, until soft. Add celery and carrot; cook, stirring, about 5 minutes or until vegetables are browned. Add chicken bones, lime leaves and the water; bring to boil. Simmer, uncovered, 2 hours.

2  Strain chicken mixture through muslin-lined sieve over large bowl. Discard solids; reserve stock. *[Best made ahead to this stage. Cover; freeze or refrigerate overnight.]*

3  Heat remaining oil in small saucepan, add finely chopped brown onion, ginger and garlic; cook, stirring, until onion is soft.

4  Combine cooled onion mixture in large bowl with chicken and finely chopped green onion. Roll level tablespoons of chicken mixture into dumpling shapes, cover; refrigerate 30 minutes. *[Can be made ahead to this stage. Cover; refrigerate overnight or freeze.]*

5  Reheat stock in large saucepan; when stock is simmering, add dumplings. Simmer, covered, about 10 minutes or until dumplings are cooked through.

6  Just before serving, stir through extra green onion, sprouts and sauce.

SERVES 8

**per serve**  6.8g fat; 883kJ

**serving suggestion**  Start a Chinese meal with this soup.

**tip**  Use a whole chicken instead of the chicken bones when making the stock; shred the cooked meat before adding it to the soup.

*Rolling tablespoons of dumpling mixture*

*Adding dumplings to simmering stock*

# chicken and borlotti bean casserole

*You need to buy approximately 1kg of unshelled fresh borlotti beans for this recipe.*

**16 chicken thigh cutlets (2.5kg)**
**1/4 cup plain flour (35g)**
**2 tablespoons olive oil**
**2 medium brown onions (300g), chopped finely**
**2 cloves garlic, crushed**
**1 tablespoon finely grated lemon rind**
**11/2 tablespoons sugar**
**500g fennel, sliced thinly**
**1/2 cup dry white wine (125ml)**
**400g can tomatoes**
**1/2 cup tomato paste (125g)**
**2 cups chicken stock (500ml)**
**4 cups shelled fresh borlotti beans (550g)**
**1/2 cup coarsely chopped fresh curly parsley**

1 Remove and discard skin from chicken; toss chicken in flour, shaking away excess. Heat oil in large heavy-base saucepan; cook chicken, in batches, until browned all over. Drain on absorbent paper.

2 Add onion, garlic, rind and 1 tablespoon of the sugar to same pan; cook, stirring, over low heat about 5 minutes or until onion is caramelised.

3 Add fennel; cook, stirring, 5 minutes. Add wine; cook, stirring, about 5 minutes or until wine is reduced by half. Stir in undrained crushed tomatoes, paste, stock, remaining sugar and chicken; bring to boil. Simmer chicken mixture, covered, 30 minutes. Add beans; simmer, covered, about 1 hour or until beans are tender. *[Can be frozen, as is or in portions, covered, at this stage.]*

4 Just before serving, stir in parsley.

SERVES 8

**per serve** 14.8g fat; 1735kJ
**serving suggestion** Serve with creamy warm polenta.

*Slicing only the bulb of the fennel*

*Shelling the fresh borlotti beans*

# moroccan couscous-filled chicken

*If you intend eating one chicken straightaway and freezing the other, only use half the ingredients that make up the couscous mixture now, and the same amount again when you thaw the frozen chicken. The couscous mixture must be used fresh, not frozen.*

**1/2 cup coarsely chopped
    fresh oregano**
**2 tablespoons finely grated
    lemon rind**
**2 tablespoons lemon juice**
**1/2 cup olive oil (125ml)**
**2 cloves garlic, crushed**
**2 teaspoons cracked black pepper**
**2 x No. 15 chickens (3kg)**
**1 1/2 cups couscous (300g)**
**1 cup boiling water (250ml)**
**40g butter**
**1 tablespoon peanut oil**
**1 medium red onion (170g),
    chopped coarsely**
**1/3 cup shelled pistachios
    (50g), toasted**
**2 tablespoons coarsely chopped
    fresh oregano, extra**
**2 tablespoons drained, coarsely
    chopped preserved lemon**

1  Combine oregano, rind, juice, olive oil, garlic and pepper in small jug; mix well.

2  Place each whole chicken in a large glass bowl. Divide marinade between the two bowls; turn chicken until coated thoroughly with marinade. Cover bowls separately; refrigerate overnight. *[Can be frozen as is, chickens covered separately, at this stage.]*

3  Place couscous and the water in medium heatproof bowl, cover; stand about 5 minutes or until water is absorbed.

4  Meanwhile, heat butter and peanut oil in small frying pan; cook onion, stirring, until soft. Add onion mixture to couscous with nuts, extra oregano and preserved lemon; mix well.

5  Preheat oven to moderate. Fill chicken cavities with couscous mixture; secure with toothpicks. Tuck wings under body; tie legs together with kitchen string. Place chickens in large oiled baking dish; roast, uncovered, in moderate oven about 1 1/2 hours or until browned and cooked through. Cover chickens individually with foil halfway through cooking time if over-browning.

SERVES 8

**per serve**  27.8g fat; 1654kJ

**serving suggestions**  This recipe is delicious served with a large bowl of tabbouleh or fattoush.

**tip**  Serve the couscous mixture on the side if you prefer not to stuff the chicken.

*Chopping the preserved lemon*

# bombay-spiced chicken skewers

*Picking up skewers to enclose in plastic bag*

*Sealing bag – sharp end of skewers protruding*

*You need 24 bamboo skewers for this recipe; soak them in water for at least 1 hour before threading on the chicken, to avoid them splintering or scorching. Frozen skewers must be thawed, in the refrigerator, before grilling.*

**1 cup peanut oil (250ml)**
**4 cloves garlic, crushed**
**2 tablespoons sweet paprika**
**1 tablespoon ground cumin**
**1 tablespoon ground turmeric**
**1 tablespoon ground coriander**
**2kg chicken breast fillets, chopped coarsely**

RAITA
**2 Lebanese cucumbers (260g), seeded, chopped finely**
**200ml yogurt**
**1 tablespoon lemon juice**
**2 cloves garlic, crushed**
**¼ cup finely chopped fresh mint leaves**

1  Heat oil in small saucepan; cook garlic and spices, stirring, until fragrant.

2  Cut chicken into 3cm pieces; thread onto 24 skewers. Place skewers in large shallow dish or oven tray, pour over spiced oil mixture; turn skewers to coat well. Combine six skewers and about one-quarter of the spiced oil mixture in each of four large freezer bags, securing tightly; having the pointed skewer ends protruding from the top of the bag so as not to pierce the plastic. Refrigerate 3 hours or overnight. *[Can be frozen, in four 6-skewer portions, at this stage.]*

3  Remove skewers from each plastic bag, shaking off excess spiced oil mixture; discard any remaining in bag. Cook skewers, in batches, on heated oiled grill plate (or grill or barbecue) until browned and cooked through. Serve skewers with raita.

**raita**  Combine ingredients in small bowl. *[Can be made ahead to this stage. Cover; refrigerate 3 hours or overnight.]*

SERVES 8

**per serve**  14.7g fat; 1614kJ
**serving suggestion**  Serve with steamed cinnamon-scented basmati rice.
**tip**  Chicken thigh fillets can be used instead of breast fillets.

# thai duck curry

*This recipe can easily be halved to make two separate meals, each serving four people. To do so, make the curry sauce and freeze in two equal portions. To serve, thaw one portion of curry sauce and add 2 Chinese barbecued ducks – fresh, not frozen. Simmer until heated through.*

**¼ cup raw peanuts (35g)**
**2 teaspoons ground cumin**
**1 teaspoon coriander seeds**
**¼ cup coarsely chopped**
　**fresh lemon grass**
**5 cloves garlic, quartered**
**1 teaspoon shrimp paste**
**5 red Thai chillies, quartered**
**1 tablespoon coarsely chopped**
　**fresh coriander root**
**2 tablespoons lime juice**
**1 tablespoon coarsely grated**
　**kaffir lime rind**
**2 tablespoons coarsely chopped**
　**purple shallots**
**1 tablespoon coarsely grated**
　**fresh galangal**
**1 tablespoon water**
**3 cups coconut cream (750ml)**
**½ cup fish sauce (125ml)**
**½ cup coarsely chopped**
　**palm sugar (135g)**
**⅔ cup water (160ml), extra**
**4 Chinese barbecued ducks,**
　**chopped, boned**

1　In heated small frying pan, toast nuts, cumin and seeds, stirring, until nuts are just browned. Blend or process nut mixture with lemon grass, garlic, paste, chilli, coriander root, juice, rind, shallots, galangal and the water until mixture forms a paste. *[Can be refrigerated overnight or frozen, covered, at this stage.]*

2　Add half of the coconut cream to large saucepan; bring to boil. Add curry paste; simmer, uncovered, until mixture is reduced by half. Add sauce and sugar; simmer, uncovered, about 5 minutes or until sugar dissolves. Stir in remaining cream and the extra water; simmer, uncovered, 5 minutes. *[Curry sauce can be frozen, covered, as is or in portions, at this stage.]*

3　Add meat from ducks to pan containing curry sauce; simmer, uncovered, until heated through.

SERVES 8

**per serve**  58.9g fat; 3079kJ

**serving suggestion**  Serve with steamed jasmine rice and cucumber spears.

**tip**  If you buy the barbecued ducks, already chopped, from an Asian barbecue shop, pick over the meat carefully to remove any bones.

• Use an equivalent weight of barbecued chicken in place of the duck.

*Toasting nuts, cumin and seeds*

*The finished processed curry paste*

# chicken and prosciutto cannelloni

*Cutting the prosciutto crossways*

*Rolling the filled pasta sheets*

50g butter
1/4 cup plain flour (35g)
2/3 cup milk (160ml)
11/2 cups chicken stock (375ml)
1/2 cup finely grated
   parmesan cheese (40g)
400g fontina cheese,
   grated coarsely
1 tablespoon olive oil
2 medium brown onions
   (300g), chopped
3 cloves garlic, crushed
1kg chicken mince
2 tablespoons chopped
   fresh sage leaves
4 x 400g cans tomatoes
1/2 cup dry white wine (125ml)
1/4 cup tomato paste (60g)
3 teaspoons sugar
12 fresh lasagne sheets
24 slices prosciutto (360g)

1 Heat butter in medium
saucepan, add flour; cook,
stirring, until flour thickens and
bubbles. Gradually stir in milk
and stock; cook, stirring, until
sauce boils and thickens. Remove
from heat; stir in parmesan and
one-quarter of the fontina.

2 Heat oil in large saucepan; cook
onion and garlic, stirring, until
onion is soft. Add chicken; cook,
stirring, until browned, stir
in sage. Combine chicken and
cheese sauce in large bowl; cool.

3 Combine undrained crushed
tomatoes, wine, paste and sugar
in same large pan; cook, stirring,
10 minutes. Cool 10 minutes;
blend or process, in batches,
until smooth.

4 Cut pasta sheets and prosciutto
slices in half crossways. Place
2 pieces prosciutto on each
piece of pasta; top each with
1/4-cup chicken mixture, roll to
enclose filling. Repeat with
remaining pasta, prosciutto
and chicken mixture.

5 If baking cannelloni now, preheat
oven to moderate. Oil two 3-litre
(12-cup) ovenproof dishes.

6 Pour one-quarter of the tomato
sauce into base of one prepared
dish; place half of the pasta
rolls, seam-side down, in dish.
Pour one-third of the remaining
tomato sauce over rolls; sprinkle
with half of the remaining
fontina cheese. Repeat process
in second dish with remaining
rolls, sauce and cheese. *[Can
be frozen, covered separately,
at this stage.]*

7 Bake cannelloni, covered, in
moderate oven 30 minutes;
uncover, bake 15 minutes
or until cheese is melted
and browned.

SERVES 8

**per serve** 37.5g fat; 2998kJ
**serving suggestion** Serve with
a simple mixed leaf salad with
lemon juice and oil dressing.

**tips** Prosciutto can be
substituted with pancetta
or double-smoked ham.

• You can also add a small
sage leaf to each pasta parcel
before rolling.

# chicken pancetta ragout

**2kg chicken thigh cutlets**
**2 tablespoons olive oil**
**12 slices pancetta**
**2 medium brown onions (300g), sliced**
**2 cloves garlic, crushed**
**2 x 400g cans tomatoes**
**1/3 cup tomato paste (80g)**
**1 cup dry white wine (250ml)**
**2 cups chicken stock (500ml)**
**2 medium carrots (240g), chopped coarsely**
**1/3 cup finely chopped fresh flat-leaf parsley**

1 Remove and discard skin from chicken.

2 Heat half of the oil in large saucepan; cook chicken, in batches, until browned.

3 Cut pancetta slices in half. Heat remaining oil in same pan; cook onion, garlic and pancetta, stirring, until pancetta is browned.

4 Add undrained crushed tomatoes, paste, wine and stock; bring to boil. Simmer, uncovered, 30 minutes. Add carrot; simmer about 30 minutes or until carrot is tender. *[Can be frozen, as is or in portions, covered, at this stage. If freezing at this stage, you may need to add extra stock when reheating.]* Stir through parsley just before serving.

SERVES 8

**per serve**  17.4g fat; 1658kJ

**serving suggestions**  Serve with steamed tiny new potatoes or a plain short pasta such as penne.

*Removing skin from chicken*

*Cutting pancetta slices in half*

# barbecued sweet-and-spicy quail

*Each portion of frozen quail must be defrosted completely before being grilled.*

**24 quails**
**2 cups mango chutney (540g)**
**2 tablespoons cumin seeds**
**1 tablespoon sweet paprika**
**1 tablespoon coarsely grated lemon rind**
**1 cup lemon juice (250ml)**
**1 teaspoon cracked black pepper**
**4 cloves garlic, crushed**
**1/2 cup coarsely chopped fresh coriander leaves**

1 Remove and discard necks from quails. Cut along both sides of each quail's backbone; discard backbone. Halve each quail along the breastbone.

2 Combine chutney, cumin, paprika, rind, juice, pepper and garlic in large bowl; reserve 1/2 cup of marinade (125ml).

3 Stir 1 tablespoon of the coriander leaves into reserved marinade, cover; refrigerate. Stir remaining coriander into marinade in bowl; add all the quails, mix well. Cover; refrigerate overnight. *[Can be frozen, as is or in portions, covered separately, at this stage.]*

4 Cook quails, in batches, on heated oiled grill plate (or grill or barbecue) until browned and cooked through. Serve with reserved marinade.

SERVES 8

**per serve**  45.8g fat; 3536kJ
**serving suggestions**  Serve with cucumber and mint salad.
**tip**  Use this marinade for chicken pieces or butterflied spatchcock, if preferred.

*Removing quail's backbone*

*Cutting quail in half along breastbone*

# chicken ravioli with tarragon sauce

*Frozen ravioli can be cooked without thawing first.*

**750g chicken mince**
**2 green onions, sliced finely**
**2 teaspoons finely grated lemon rind**
**56 gow gee wrappers**
**1 egg, beaten lightly**
**2 teaspoons olive oil**
**1 medium brown onion (150g), chopped finely**
**2 cloves garlic, crushed**
**1/2 cup dry white wine (125ml)**
**1 tablespoon Dijon mustard**
**600ml cream**
**2 tablespoons coarsely chopped fresh tarragon leaves**

1   Combine chicken, green onion and rind in medium bowl.

2   Brush 1 wrapper at a time with egg. Place a rounded teaspoon of
    the chicken mixture in centre of wrapper; fold over to enclose filling,
    press edge to seal. Repeat with remaining wrappers, egg and
    chicken mixture. Place ravioli, in single layer, on tray, cover;
    refrigerate 30 minutes. *[Can be frozen, as is or in portions,
    covered, at this stage.]*

3   Meanwhile, heat oil in medium saucepan; cook brown onion and
    garlic, stirring, until onion is just browned. Add wine; cook, stirring,
    about 5 minutes or until wine is reduced by half. Stir in mustard and
    cream; cook sauce, stirring, until up to the boil.

4   Meanwhile, cook ravioli, uncovered, in large saucepan of boiling water
    until each ravioli floats to the top; drain. Return ravioli to same pan;
    add tarragon and cream sauce, toss gently to combine.

SERVES 8

**per serve**   38.5g fat; 2233kJ

**serving suggestion**   Serve with a side dish of crisp, steamed green
vegetables – try baby zucchini.

*Folding wrapper over filling*

*Pulling tarragon leaves off stem*

# vietnamese spring rolls

*Frozen spring rolls can be deep-fried.*

**1 medium red capsicum (200g)**
**1 medium carrot (120g)**
**1 tablespoon peanut oil**
**700g chicken breast fillets**
**100g bean thread noodles**
**1 tablespoon grated fresh ginger**
**2 cloves garlic, crushed**
**4 green onions, chopped finely**
**1 tablespoon finely chopped fresh**
**    Vietnamese mint leaves**
**500g bok choy, shredded finely**
**1/4 cup sweet chilli sauce (60ml)**
**1 tablespoon soy sauce**
**40 spring roll wrappers**
**peanut oil, for deep-frying**

DIPPING SAUCE

**1/3 cup sweet chilli**
**    sauce (80ml)**
**2 tablespoons lime juice**
**3 green onions, chopped finely**

1 Halve capsicum; discard seeds and membrane. Slice capsicum and carrot into paper-thin strips.

2 Heat half of the oil in medium saucepan; cook chicken, in batches, until browned and cooked through. Cool 10 minutes; shred finely.

3 Meanwhile, place noodles in large heatproof bowl; cover with boiling water, stand 2 minutes. Drain noodles; chop roughly. Heat remaining oil in same pan; cook ginger, garlic and onion, stirring, about 2 minutes or until onion is soft.

4 Combine carrot, capsicum, chicken, noodles and onion mixture in large bowl with mint, bok choy and sauces. *[Can be made ahead to this stage. Cover; refrigerate overnight.]*

5 Place rounded tablespoon of mixture across edge of 1 wrapper; roll to enclose filling, folding in ends. Place on tray, seam-side down. Repeat with remaining mixture and wrappers, placing on tray in single layer. *[Can be frozen, as is or in portions, covered, at this stage.]*

6 Just before serving, heat oil in wok or large deep-frying pan; deep-fry spring rolls, in batches, until golden brown and cooked through. Drain on absorbent paper; serve with dipping sauce.

**dipping sauce** Combine ingredients in small bowl. *[Can be made ahead to this stage. Cover; refrigerate overnight or freeze, as is or in portions.]*

SERVES 8 (MAKES 40)

**per serve** 21.5g fat; 1535kJ

**serving suggestion** Use finely chopped raw Thai chillies mixed with brown vinegar to make an alternative dipping sauce with more kick.

**tip** Freeze spring rolls, in single layer, between sheets of plastic wrap. This makes it easier to remove and defrost small quantities at a time.

*Shredding chicken finely*

*Rolling spring rolls to enclose filling*

# chicken and preserved lemon tagine

*Smashing olives*

*Adding preserved lemon to tagine*

**2 x No. 18 chickens (3.6kg)**
**1/4 cup olive oil (60ml)**
**2 medium brown onions (300g), chopped coarsely**
**2 teaspoons ground cumin**
**pinch saffron threads**
**2 teaspoons ground coriander**
**1 teaspoon sweet paprika**
**1/2 teaspoon ground cinnamon**
**1 tablespoon grated fresh ginger**
**4 cloves garlic, crushed**
**1 tablespoon plain flour**
**1.5 litres chicken stock (6 cups)**
**400g large green olives**
**2/3 cup drained preserved lemon slices (140g)**
**1/3 cup finely chopped fresh flat-leaf parsley**

1  Cut each chicken into eight pieces. Heat half of the oil in large saucepan; cook chicken, in batches, until well browned.

2  Heat remaining oil in same pan; cook onion, spices, ginger and garlic, stirring, until onion is soft and spices fragrant. Add flour; cook, stirring, until mixture bubbles.

3  Gradually stir in stock; cook, stirring, until mixture boils. Return chicken to pan, simmer, covered, about 40 minutes or until chicken is tender and cooked through. *[Can be frozen, as is or in portions, covered, at this stage.]*

4  Smash olives with flat side of large knife or cleaver; discard seeds. Add olives, lemon and parsley; simmer tagine until heated through.

SERVES 8

**per serve**  43.9g fat; 2688kJ

**serving suggestion**  Serve with almond and coriander couscous.

tip  You can use approximately 3.5kg of any chicken piece on the bone you like (thighs, drumsticks, etc) rather than the whole birds in this recipe.

# beef and veal

You can serve a meat-based main course that's far more interesting than just a few grilled chops. These soups, stews and casseroles can be thawed in the refrigerator during the day then quickly reheated for dinner.

## chunky beef and vegetable soup

**1 cup black-eye beans (200g)**
**1 tablespoon olive oil**
**2 medium brown onions (300g), chopped coarsely**
**1.5kg gravy beef, trimmed, chopped into 2cm pieces**
**4 litres beef stock (16 cups)**
**4 trimmed celery sticks (300g), chopped coarsely**
**4 medium carrots (480g), chopped coarsely**

1 Place beans in medium bowl, cover with water, soak overnight; drain.

2 Heat oil in large saucepan; cook onion, stirring, until soft, remove from pan. Add beef to pan, in batches; cook, stirring, until browned all over.

3 Add beans, onion and stock to pan, bring to a boil; simmer, covered, about 40 minutes or until beans are tender, skimming surface occasionally.

4 Add vegetables; simmer, covered, about 20 minutes or until vegetables are tender. *[Can be frozen, as is or in portions, at this stage.]*

SERVES 8

**per serve** 15.7g fat; 1838kJ

**tip** Any dried bean can be substituted for the black-eye beans but, because some take longer than others to cook, cooking times will differ.

*Trimming fat and sinew from gravy beef*

*Skimming excess fat from soup surface*

# satay beef with aromatic rice

*You will need 24 bamboo skewers for this recipe; soak them in water for at least an hour to avoid them splintering when you thread on the meat. Beef skewers must be thawed before being grilled.*

**2 tablespoons ground cumin**
**2 tablespoons ground coriander**
**1 tablespoon ground turmeric**
**4 red Thai chillies, chopped finely**
**2 tablespoons finely chopped
  lemon grass**
**2 tablespoons grated fresh ginger**
**4 cloves garlic, crushed**
**1/3 cup peanut oil (80ml)**
**2kg beef sirloin steak,
  sliced thinly**
**3 cups water (750ml)**
**2 cups coconut cream (500ml)**
**3 cups jasmine rice (600g)**
**6 kaffir lime leaves,
  shredded finely**
**1 cup crunchy peanut butter (260g)**
**1 cup coconut milk (250ml)**
**1/2 cup beef stock (125ml)**
**2 tablespoons brown sugar**
**2 tablespoons lemon juice**
**1/4 cup coarsely chopped
  fresh coriander**

1 Combine spices, chilli, lemon grass, ginger, garlic and oil in large bowl; add beef, stir to coat with spice mixture.

2 Thread beef onto 24 skewers, patting any spice mixture remaining in bowl onto beef once skewered. Cover; refrigerate 3 hours or overnight. *[Can be frozen, in four 6-skewer portions, at this stage.]*

3 Bring the water and coconut cream to a boil in large heavy-base saucepan; add rice and lime leaves. Simmer, uncovered, until rice is just tender; drain. Pack rice firmly into eight 3/4-cup oiled timbales or soufflé dishes. *[Can be made ahead to this stage. Cover; refrigerate overnight.]*

4 Meanwhile, combine peanut butter, coconut milk, stock, sugar and juice in medium saucepan; cook, stirring, about 5 minutes or until sauce thickens. *[Can be made ahead to this stage. Cover; refrigerate overnight.]*

5 Cook skewers on heated oiled grill plate (or grill or barbecue) until browned all over and cooked as desired. Stir coriander into hot satay sauce; serve with rice and skewers.

SERVES 8

**per serve** 62g fat; 4996kJ

**serving suggestion** Serve with deep-fried rice crackers and fresh cucumber spears.

**tip** You can use pork loin or chicken thigh fillets, chopped into pieces, instead of the beef if you prefer.

*Chopping white half of lemon grass stalks*

*Turning the rice out of the moulds to serve*

# piroshki

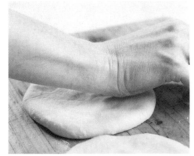
*Pressing dough into 12cm rounds*

*Pinching dough to enclose filling*

6 cups plain flour (900g)
1 tablespoon dry yeast
1 tablespoon salt
1/3 cup sugar (75g)
2 egg yolks
2 cups milk (500ml), warmed
250g butter, melted
1 egg, beaten lightly

FILLING

1 tablespoon olive oil
1 medium brown onion (150g), chopped finely
1 clove garlic, crushed
150g button mushrooms, sliced thinly
2 bacon rashers, chopped finely
400g minced beef
1/3 cup tomato paste (90g)
2 teaspoons fresh thyme leaves

1 Combine flour, yeast, salt and sugar in large bowl. Make a well in the centre; using hand, mix in egg yolks, milk and butter until mixture is soft and elastic. Scrape down sides of bowl, cover; stand in warm place about 1 hour or until dough doubles in size.

2 Turn dough onto floured surface; knead until smooth. Divide dough into 16 pieces; press each piece into 12cm round.

3 Preheat oven to hot. Place rounded tablespoon of cooled filling in centre of each round; gather edges, pinch firmly to enclose filling. Place piroshki, pinched-side down, on lightly oiled trays; brush with egg. Stand, uncovered, in warm place 15 minutes.

4 Bake piroshki, uncovered, in hot oven about 15 minutes or until golden brown. *[Can be frozen, as is or in portions, covered, at this stage.]*

**filling** Heat oil in large frying pan, cook onion, garlic, mushrooms and bacon, stirring, until onion is soft and mixture is dry. Add beef; cook, stirring, until beef changes colour, stir in paste and thyme.

SERVES 8

**per serve** 40.7g fat; 3646kJ

**serving suggestion** Piroshki make fabulous hors d'oeuvre.

tips Vary the filling: try adding chopped roasted eggplant, capsicum and onion.

• Reheat piroshki briefly in microwave oven or in preheated hot oven for 10 minutes.

# braised beef curry with dhal

1 tablespoon peanut oil
2 medium brown onions (300g),
　chopped coarsely
2 cloves garlic, crushed
1 red Thai chilli, chopped finely
1 tablespoon grated fresh ginger
2 teaspoons garam masala
2 tablespoons ground cumin
2 tablespoons ground coriander
2 teaspoons hot paprika
4 cardamom pods, bruised
3 cinnamon sticks, broken
2 cups water (500ml)
2kg beef chuck steak,
　cut into 2cm pieces
3 cups beef stock (750ml)
1/2 cup coconut milk (125ml)
1/3 cup finely chopped fresh
　coriander leaves
3 cups red lentils (600g)

1 Heat oil in large heavy-base saucepan; cook onion, garlic, chilli and ginger, stirring, until onion is soft. Stir in spices; cook, stirring, until fragrant.

2 Gradually stir 1/2 cup of the water into onion mixture until it forms a paste; cook, stirring, 2 minutes. Add beef; stir to coat in paste.

3 Add remaining water and stock; bring to a boil. Simmer, covered, stirring occasionally, about 11/2 hours or until beef is tender. *[Can be frozen as is, covered, at this stage.]*

4 Add coconut milk; simmer, uncovered, about 30 minutes or until thickened slightly. Stir in coriander.

5 Meanwhile, cook lentils in medium saucepan of boiling water, uncovered, about 10 minutes or until tender; drain. Serve lentils with curry.

SERVES 8

**per serve** 20.1g fat; 2516kJ

**serving suggestion** Accompany this curry with a banana and chilli raita.

**tip** If you want to eat this curry without freezing, make it the day before through to the end of step 3, refrigerating it overnight to allow the flavours to develop.

*Bruising cardamom with a heavy knife*

*Adding water to onion mixture*

# empanadas

*These South American/Mexican meat "turnovers" get their name from the Spanish word* empanar, *which means to bake in pastry. Empanadas can be individual-size, as we show here, or large enough to feed a family.*

*Cutting out the rounds of pastry*

*Pressing edges together to seal*

**400g can tomatoes**
**1 tablespoon olive oil**
**1 medium brown onion (150g), chopped finely**
**1 clove garlic, crushed**
**1 teaspoon cracked black pepper**
**1/2 teaspoon ground cinnamon**
**1/2 teaspoon ground clove**
**600g minced beef**
**1/4 cup raisins (40g), chopped coarsely**
**1 tablespoon cider vinegar**
**1/4 cup toasted slivered almonds (35g)**
**2 x 800g packages ready-rolled quiche pastry**
**1 egg, beaten lightly**
**vegetable oil, for deep-frying**

1  Blend or process undrained tomatoes until smooth; reserve.

2  Heat oil in large heavy-base saucepan; cook onion, garlic and spices, stirring, until onion is soft. Add beef; cook, stirring, until changed in colour. Drain away excess fat from pan. Stir in tomato, raisins and vinegar; simmer, uncovered, about 20 minutes or until filling mixture thickens. Stir in almonds. *[Can be frozen as is, covered, at this stage.]*

3  Cut 9cm rounds from each pastry sheet (you will get 32 rounds). Place a level tablespoon of beef mixture in centre of each round; brush edge lightly with egg. Fold pastry over to enclose filling, press edges together to seal. *[Can be frozen, as is or in portions, covered, at this stage.]*

4  Heat oil in large deep-frying pan; deep-fry empanadas until crisp and browned lightly, drain on absorbent paper. Serve immediately with a dollop of sour cream or bottled salsa, if desired.

SERVES 8

**per serve**  26g fat; 1664kJ

**serving suggestion**  Spanish rice and refried beans make perfect accompaniments to empanadas.

tip  For a lower-fat version, empanadas can be baked, uncovered, in a preheated hot oven about 25 minutes or until browned.

# barbecued red wine beef

**1¹/₂ cups dry red wine (375ml)**
**¹/₂ cup beef stock (125ml)**
**2 tablespoons olive oil**
**¹/₂ cup finely shredded fresh
    basil leaves**
**3 cloves garlic, crushed**
**8 beef rib steaks (2.4kg)**
**8 medium potatoes (1.6kg),
    chopped coarsely**
**³/₄ cup buttermilk (180ml)**
**¹/₂ cup finely grated parmesan
    cheese (40g)**

1 Combine wine, stock, oil, basil and garlic with beef in large bowl;
  stir to coat beef in marinade. Cover; refrigerate 3 hours or overnight.
  *[Can be frozen in pairs, covered, at this stage.]*

2 Preheat oven to hot. Boil, steam or microwave potato until tender;
  drain. Mash potatoes in large bowl, with buttermilk and cheese, until
  smooth; cover to keep warm.

3 Drain beef over large bowl; reserve marinade. Cook beef, in batches, on
  heated oiled grill plate (or grill or barbecue) about 5 minutes each side
  or until browned. Transfer beef to oven trays; cook, uncovered, in hot
  oven about 10 minutes or until cooked as desired.

4 Meanwhile, place reserved marinade in small saucepan; bring to a boil.
  Simmer, uncovered, about 10 minutes or until sauce thickens. Serve
  warm mash with beef and sauce.

SERVES 8

**per serve**  29.2g fat; 2694kJ

**serving suggestion**  Serve with baby spinach leaves and grilled
cherry tomatoes.

**tips**  Marinate beef in the same wine you plan to serve with the meal.

● Freeze in batches of 2 steaks per freezer bag: they will freeze faster this
way and ice crystals will be prevented from forming.

*Bagging steaks with the marinade in pairs*          *Finishing the cooking of steaks in oven*

# american meatloaf with caramelised onion

*Thinly slicing onion*

*Shaping meat mixture into a loaf*

2 medium brown onions
   (300g), chopped coarsely
2 large carrots (360g),
   chopped coarsely
2 trimmed celery sticks (150g),
   chopped coarsely
2 cloves garlic, quartered
2 cups packaged
   breadcrumbs (200g)
1 teaspoon salt
1 tablespoon mustard powder
1.5kg minced beef
3 eggs, beaten lightly
2 tablespoons mild chilli sauce
1/4 cup barbecue sauce (60ml)
1 cup tomato sauce (250ml)
40g butter
6 medium brown onions (900g),
   sliced thinly, extra
1/3 cup firmly packed
   brown sugar (75g)
1/3 cup cider vinegar (80ml)

1 Preheat oven to moderate.

2 Blend or process onion, carrot,
celery and garlic until chopped
finely; place in large bowl. Add
breadcrumbs, salt, mustard
powder, beef, eggs and half of
each sauce; using hands, mix
until just combined.

3 Divide mixture in half; place
each half on lightly oiled Swiss
roll pans, form each half into
a 10cm x 30cm loaf shape.

4 Brush top of each meatloaf with
half of the remaining combined
sauces. Bake in moderate oven,
uncovered, brushing meatloaf
tops occasionally with remaining
combined sauces, about 1 hour
or until cooked through. *[Can
be frozen, individually covered,
at this stage.]*

5 Meanwhile, melt butter in large
heavy-base saucepan; cook
extra onion, stirring, about
10 minutes or until onion is soft
and browned lightly. Stir in
sugar and vinegar; cook,
stirring, about 15 minutes or
until onion is caramelised.
*[Can be frozen as is or in portions,
covered, at this stage.]*

SERVES 8

**per serve** 18.7g fat; 2336kJ
**serving suggestion** Serve with
mashed potatoes.

tip Leftover cold meatloaf is
great, with seeded mustard and
lettuce, sandwiched between
bread slices.

# chile con carne with jalapeño corn muffins

1 cup dried kidney beans (200g)
1.5kg beef chuck steak
2 litres water (8 cups)
1 tablespoon olive oil
2 medium brown onions (300g),
    chopped coarsely
2 cloves garlic, crushed
2 teaspoons ground cumin
2 teaspoons ground coriander
1/2 teaspoon ground
    cayenne pepper
2 teaspoons sweet paprika
2 x 400g cans tomatoes
1 tablespoon tomato paste
4 green onions, chopped coarsely
2 tablespoons finely chopped
    fresh coriander leaves
1/3 cup finely chopped, bottled
    jalapeño chillies (65g)

JALAPEÑO CORN MUFFINS

1 cup plain flour (150g)
1 teaspoon baking powder
2 cups polenta (340g)
2 teaspoons salt
1 cup milk (250ml)
2 cups buttermilk (500ml)
2 tablespoons olive oil
2 eggs, beaten lightly
1 1/3 cups finely grated cheddar
    cheese (165g)
1/3 cup finely chopped, bottled
    jalapeño chillies (65g)

1 Place beans in medium bowl,
  cover with water; soak
  overnight, drain.

2 Combine beef with the water
  in large saucepan; bring to
  a boil; simmer, covered,
  1 1/2 hours, cool slightly.

3 Drain meat in large muslin-lined
  strainer placed over bowl; reserve
  3 1/2 cups of the cooking liquid.
  Using two forks, shred beef.

4 Heat oil in same pan; cook
  brown onion and garlic, stirring,
  until onion is soft. Add spices;
  cook, stirring, until fragrant.
  Add beans, undrained crushed
  tomatoes, paste and 2 cups
  of the reserved cooking liquid;
  bring to a boil. Simmer,
  covered, 1 hour.

5 Add beef and remaining
  cooking liquid to pan; simmer,
  covered, about 30 minutes or
  until beans are tender. [Can
  be frozen, as is or in portions,
  covered, at this stage.]

6 Just before serving, stir in green
  onion, coriander and chilli.
  Serve chile con carne with
  jalapeño corn muffins.

**jalapeño corn muffins** Preheat
oven to moderate. Sift flour and
baking powder into large bowl;
add remaining ingredients, mix
until just combined. Spoon corn
muffin mixture into a 12-hole
(1/2-cup capacity) muffin pan.
Bake, uncovered, in moderate
oven 35 minutes. [Can be
frozen, individually covered,
at this stage.]

SERVES 8

**per serve** chile con carne
11.7g fat; 1290kJ

muffins 16.7g fat; 1715kJ

**serving suggestion** Corn
chips and guacamole are good
served beforehand.

**tips** If you can find fresh
jalapeño chillies, use 2 in both
the chile and the muffins, seeded
and chopped finely.

• Use chile con carne as a
burrito filling: enclose heated
chile in large flour tortillas;
top with grated cheddar,
guacamole and sour cream.

• Reheat any leftover corn
muffins wrapped in foil in
moderate oven about 15 minutes.

*Shredding the beef using two forks*

*Crushing canned tomatoes in the pan*

# beef turnovers

**1 tablespoon olive oil**
**2 medium brown onions (300g), chopped coarsely**
**800g minced beef**
**2 medium carrots (240g), chopped coarsely**
**¼ cup plain flour (35g)**
**3 cups beef stock (750ml)**
**1½ cups frozen peas (185g)**
**1 cup frozen corn kernels (140g)**
**6 sheets ready-rolled puff pastry**
**1 egg, beaten lightly**

1 Heat oil in large heavy-base saucepan; cook onion, stirring, until soft. Add beef; cook, stirring, until beef changes colour. Add carrot, and blended flour and stock; cook, stirring, until filling mixture boils and thickens. Stir in peas and corn; cool. *[Can be made ahead to this stage and refrigerated, covered, overnight.]*

2 Cut six 18cm rounds from pastry. Join pastry scraps; cut two more 18cm rounds.

3 Preheat oven to hot. Place one-eighth of filling in centre of each round; brush edge lightly with egg. Fold pastry over to enclose filling, press edges together to seal. Brush turnovers, both sides, with egg; place on lightly oiled oven trays. *[Can be frozen, as is or in portions, covered, at this stage.]*

4 Bake, uncovered, in hot oven about 20 minutes or until pastry is browned and turnovers are heated through.

SERVES 8

**per serve** 21.1g fat; 1635kJ

**serving suggestion** Serve with homemade tomato sauce.

**tip** Fresh peas and corn can be substituted. You will need about 500g unshelled fresh peas and 1 large fresh corn cob.

*Joining pastry scraps to make extra rounds*

*Pressing edge of turnover with fork tines*

# osso buco

*Buy osso buco pieces – often called veal shin by butchers – with the skin intact, measuring about 7cm across and 3cm in thickness.*

**1 tablespoon olive oil**
**16 pieces veal shin**
   **(approximately 3.2kg)**
**3 medium brown onions (450g),**
   **chopped coarsely**
**3 cloves garlic, crushed**
**1 tablespoon plain flour**
**1.25 litres chicken stock (5 cups)**
**1 cup dry white wine (250ml)**
**2 x 400g cans tomatoes**
**1 teaspoon dried thyme**
**1 teaspoon cracked black pepper**
**4 medium carrots (480g),**
   **chopped coarsely**
**4 trimmed celery sticks (300g),**
   **chopped coarsely**
**3 medium lemons (420g)**
**1 cup finely chopped fresh**
   **flat-leaf parsley**

1 Heat oil in large heavy-base saucepan; cook veal, in batches, until browned all over.

2 Add onion and garlic to same pan; cook, stirring, until onion is soft. Add flour; cook, stirring, 1 minute. Return veal to pan with stock, wine, undrained crushed tomatoes, thyme and pepper; bring to a boil. Simmer, uncovered, $1^{1}/_{2}$ hours.

3 Add carrot and celery; simmer, uncovered, about 30 minutes or until vegetables are tender. *[Can be frozen, as is or in portions, covered, at this stage.]*

4 Meanwhile, using lemon zester, remove rind from lemons. Combine rind with 2 tablespoons of juice from same lemons and parsley in small bowl; sprinkle over osso buco to serve.

SERVES 8

**per serve** 6.8g fat; 1661kJ

**serving suggestion** Serve with either soft creamy polenta or the traditional risotto milanese.

**tip** Frenched lamb shanks can be used instead of veal shin.

*Adding stock to pan*

*Removing lemon rind with a zester*

# mediterranean burgers

**1.5kg minced beef**
**2 teaspoons finely grated**
  **lemon rind**
**3 cloves garlic, crushed**
**1 tablespoon coarsely chopped**
  **fresh oregano leaves**
**8 medium tomatoes (1.5kg)**
**2 teaspoons balsamic vinegar**
**1/4 cup olive oil (60ml)**
**1 long loaf ciabatta**
**1 clove garlic, crushed, extra**
**200g fetta, crumbled**
**100g baby rocket leaves**

1 Using hands, combine beef, rind, garlic and oregano in large bowl; shape meat mixture into eight patties. Place patties on tray, cover; refrigerate 30 minutes. *[Can be frozen as is or in portions, covered, at this stage.]*

2 Meanwhile, preheat oven to hot. Halve tomatoes; cut each half into three wedges. Place wedges on lightly oiled oven tray; drizzle with combined vinegar and 1 tablespoon of the oil. Roast, uncovered, in hot oven about 25 minutes or until tomato is browned and softened. *[Can be frozen as is or in portions, covered, at this stage.]*

3 Cook patties, in batches, on heated oiled grill plate (or grill or barbecue) until browned both sides and cooked through. Cover burgers to keep warm.

4 Cut bread into 16 slices, brush with combined remaining oil and extra garlic; cook bread, in batches, on same heated oiled grill plate until browned both sides.

5 Sandwich each patty with tomato, fetta and rocket between two pieces of grilled bread.

SERVES 8

**per serve** 34.8g fat; 2792kJ

**serving suggestion** Serve with spicy oven-baked potato wedges.

**tip** Add some homemade roasted capsicum, caramelised onion and basil pesto to the burger.

• Uncooked patties can be frozen, in single layer, in snap-lock plastic bags.

*Packaging uncooked patties for freezing*

*Packaging roasted tomatoes for freezing*

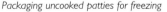

# lamb

Your freezer will become one of your favourite kitchen tools on one of those nights when you crave the taste of Indian or Moroccan food and there's no time to cook... just defrost, heat and enjoy.

## chermoulla lamb with roasted beetroot puree

*Trimming cutlet bones of all fat and sinew*

*Wearing kitchen gloves to peel beetroot*

1/2 cup olive oil (125ml)
1 medium red onion (170g),
   chopped finely
2 cloves garlic, crushed
1 tablespoon ground cumin
1 tablespoon ground coriander
2 teaspoons ground turmeric
2 teaspoons sweet paprika
1 tablespoon finely grated
   lemon rind
1/4 cup coarsely chopped fresh
   coriander leaves
1/4 cup coarsely chopped fresh
   flat-leaf parsley
1/4 cup lemon juice (60ml)
32 lamb cutlets (approximately
   2.5kg), trimmed
2kg bunch beetroot
   (approximately 6 medium)
2/3 cup sour cream (160ml)

1 Heat oil in large heavy-base saucepan; cook onion and garlic, stirring, until onion is soft. Add spices; cook, stirring, until fragrant. Stir in rind; cool. Combine onion mixture in large bowl with herbs, juice and lamb; stir to coat lamb in marinade. Cover; refrigerate 3 hours or overnight. *[Can be frozen, as is or in portions, covered, at this stage.]*

2 Preheat oven to hot. Trim beetroot of leaves and stems, leaving 2cm stem on each beetroot. Wrap beetroot individually in foil, place in large baking dish; bake in hot oven about 50 minutes or until tender. Unwrap beetroot; when cool enough to handle, peel then chop coarsely. Blend or process beetroot until smooth. *[Can be frozen, as is or in portions, covered, at this stage.]*

3 Cook lamb, in batches, on heated oiled grill plate (or grill or barbecue) until browned both sides and cooked as desired.

4 Meanwhile, reheat beetroot puree, stirring in sour cream.

SERVES 8

**per serve** 49.2g fat; 2785kJ
**serving suggestion** Serve with a mixed green salad and warm pitta.
**tip** A teaspoon of either cumin or caraway seeds, softened briefly in a little butter, can be stirred into the beetroot puree.

# harira

*This dish is a stick-to-the-ribs meat stew that has its origins in North Africa, where it is typically served at sunset during the religious month-long daylight fast of Ramadan.*

2 tablespoons olive oil
2 medium red onions (340g), chopped coarsely
1¹/₂ teaspoons ground ginger
¹/₂ teaspoon ground cinnamon
2 x 400g cans tomatoes
1.5 litres vegetable stock (6 cups)
pinch saffron threads
1kg diced lamb
1 cup long-grain white rice (200g)
1 cup red lentils (200g)
2 x 400g cans chickpeas, rinsed, drained
1kg frozen broad beans, thawed, peeled
¹/₂ cup coarsely chopped fresh coriander leaves
¹/₂ cup coarsely chopped fresh flat-leaf parsley

1 Heat oil in large heavy-base saucepan; cook onion, ginger and cinnamon, stirring, until onion is soft.

2 Add undrained crushed tomatoes, stock, saffron and lamb; bring to a boil. Simmer, covered, about 1¹/₂ hours or until lamb is tender. *[Can be frozen as is, covered, at this stage.]*

3 Add rice and lentils; simmer, uncovered, about 20 minutes or until both rice and lentils are just tender. Add chickpeas and beans; simmer, uncovered, until hot. Just before serving, stir through coriander and parsley.

SERVES 8

**per serve** 18.4g fat; 2253kJ

**serving suggestion** Drizzle this tasty stew with fresh lemon juice and accompany it with French bread.

**tip** Use fresh broad beans if in season.

*Peeling the broad beans*

*Adding rice and lentils*

# kofta kebabs with baba ghanoush

*You need 24 bamboo skewers for this recipe. Soaking them in water for at least an hour before use helps prevent them from splintering and scorching.*

**3 large eggplants (1.5kg)**
**1/3 cup tahini (80ml)**
**2 cloves garlic, quartered**
**1 tablespoon olive oil**
**2 medium brown onions (300g),**
  **chopped finely**
**2 cloves garlic, crushed, extra**
**2 tablespoons ground cumin**
**1kg minced lamb**
**2 red Thai chillies, seeded,**
  **chopped finely**
**1/4 cup finely chopped fresh**
  **flat-leaf parsley**
**2 tablespoons finely chopped**
  **fresh mint leaves**
**1 tablespoon finely grated**
  **lemon rind**
**1/2 cup lemon juice (125ml)**

1 Preheat oven to hot. Pierce eggplants all over with skewer or fork. Place whole unpeeled eggplants on oven tray; roast, uncovered, in hot oven about 1 hour or until soft.

2 When eggplants are cool enough to handle, peel by pulling off charred skin; discard skin, chop eggplant flesh coarsely. Blend or process eggplant flesh with tahini and garlic until a smooth thick puree forms. Cover; refrigerate 3 hours or overnight. *[Can be frozen as is, covered, at this stage.]*

3 Heat oil in medium saucepan; cook onion, extra garlic and cumin until onion is soft.

4 Using hand, combine cooled onion mixture in large bowl with lamb, chilli, herbs and rind; roll level tablespoons of lamb mixture into kofta "balls". Thread kofta onto skewers, place skewers on tray, cover; refrigerate at least 1 hour. *[Can be frozen, in 6-skewer portions, at this stage.]*

5 Cook kofta, in batches, on heated oiled grill plate (or grill or barbecue) until browned all over and cooked through. Stir juice into baba ghanoush before serving with kofta kebabs.

**SERVES 8**

**per serve** 23.7g fat; 1522kJ

**serving suggestion** Tabbouleh and pitta make tasty accompaniments to this dish.

**tip** Baba ghanoush freezes best without the lemon juice; stirring in the juice just before serving also helps gauge how thick or thin you serve this smoky-tasting dip-like salad.

*Piercing eggplant all over with skewer*

*Peeling away the charred eggplant skin*

# star-anise and orange lamb

*Processing star-anise and orange marinade*

*Placing lamb and orange wedges in dish*

**2 medium brown onions (300g), chopped coarsely**
**2 cloves garlic, quartered**
**4 star-anise**
**2 tablespoons coarsely grated orange rind**
**1 cup orange juice (250ml)**
**3 cups chicken stock (750ml)**
**2 x 1.5kg legs of lamb**
**2 large oranges (600g)**

1  Blend or process onion, garlic, star-anise, rind and juice until almost smooth; add stock, process briefly to just combine marinade ingredients. Divide between two large shallow flameproof baking dishes.

2  Place 1 leg of lamb in each dish, coat with orange marinade, cover; refrigerate 3 hours or overnight, turning lamb occasionally. *[Can be frozen, each leg of lamb and its marinade in a large freezer bag, sealed tightly, at this stage.]*

3  Preheat oven to moderate. Cut each orange into eight wedges; divide wedges between baking dishes.

4  Roast lamb, uncovered, in moderate oven about 1³/₄ hours, spooning marinade over lamb occasionally, until browned and cooked as desired.

5  Place lamb and orange wedges on serving platters; cover to keep warm. Bring pan juices to a boil; simmer, stirring, until reduced slightly, pour over lamb and orange to serve.

SERVES 8

**per serve**  15.3g fat; 1853kJ
**serving suggestion**  Serve with steamed jasmine rice and green beans.
**tip**  Lamb shoulders or trimmed shanks can be used instead of legs.

# hearty winter lamb casserole

**1 cup dried haricot beans (200g)**
**1 cup dried kidney beans (200g)**
**2kg lamb neck chops**
**plain flour**
**2 tablespoons olive oil**
**2 medium brown onions (300g),**
**chopped coarsely**
**2 cloves garlic, crushed**
**3 cups beef stock (750ml)**
**2 cups water (500ml)**
**1 cup dry red wine (250ml)**
**¼ cup Worcestershire**
**sauce (60ml)**
**3 trimmed celery sticks (225g),**
**chopped coarsely**
**4 large carrots (720g),**
**chopped coarsely**
**2 large parsnips (360g),**
**chopped coarsely**
**1 large swede (400g),**
**chopped coarsely**
**1 cup finely chopped fresh**
**flat-leaf parsley**

1 Place beans, separately, in medium bowls, cover with water; soak overnight, drain. Cook beans in large saucepan of boiling water until tender; drain.

2 Meanwhile, toss lamb in flour, shaking off excess. Heat half of the oil in large heavy-base saucepan; cook lamb, in batches, until browned both sides.

3 Heat remaining oil in same pan; cook onion and garlic, stirring, until onion is soft. Add lamb with stock, water, wine and sauce, bring to a boil; simmer, covered, 1 hour. Add vegetables; simmer, covered, 20 minutes. Add beans; simmer, covered, about 10 minutes or until vegetables and beans are tender. *[Can be frozen, as is or in portions, covered, at this stage.]* Just before serving, stir in parsley.

SERVES 8

**per serve**  37g fat; 3168kJ

**serving suggestion**  Serve with a robust loaf of wood-fired bread.

**tip**  If you like, stir in a few sprigs of fresh rosemary or thyme when you add the root vegetables.

*Draining beans*

*Peeling root vegetables thickly*

# lamb and ricotta ravioli

2 medium red onions (340g)
20 medium egg tomatoes
    (1.5kg), halved
2 tablespoons balsamic vinegar
1 tablespoon brown sugar
1/4 cup olive oil (60ml)
6 cloves garlic, crushed
1 litre chicken stock (4 cups)
415g can tomato puree
1/2 cup dry red wine (125ml)
500g spinach, trimmed
2 medium brown onions (300g),
    chopped finely
500g minced lamb
400g ricotta cheese
1/4 cup finely shredded fresh
    basil leaves
80 wonton wrappers (540g)
2 eggs, beaten lightly

1 Preheat oven to hot. Halve red onions; cut each half into three wedges.

2 Place onion and tomato, cut-side up, in large shallow oiled baking dishes; drizzle with vinegar then sprinkle with sugar. Bake in hot oven, uncovered, about 45 minutes or until tomato and onion are tender.

3 Heat 2 tablespoons of the oil in large saucepan; cook half of the garlic, stirring, 1 minute. Add stock, puree and wine; bring to a boil. Simmer, uncovered, about 10 minutes or until mixture thickens slightly. Stir in tomato and onion; cook, stirring, until hot. *[Can be frozen, as is or in portions, covered, at this stage.]*

4 Boil, steam or microwave spinach until just wilted; drain. Squeeze excess liquid from spinach, chop coarsely; drain on absorbent paper.

5 Meanwhile, heat remaining oil in large saucepan; cook brown onion and remaining garlic, stirring, until onion is soft. Add lamb; cook, stirring, until lamb is browned, drain away excess fat. Combine cooled lamb mixture with cheese, basil and spinach in large bowl.

6 Brush 1 wonton wrapper with egg. Place 1 level tablespoon of lamb mixture in centre of wrapper, top with another wrapper; press edges together to seal. Repeat process with remaining wrappers, egg and lamb mixture. Place ravioli, in single layer, on trays, cover; refrigerate 30 minutes. *[Can be frozen, as is or in portions, covered, at this stage.]*

7 Cook ravioli, uncovered, in two batches, in large saucepan of boiling water until they float to the top and are just tender; drain. Serve with roasted tomato sauce; top with baby basil leaves, if desired.

SERVES 8

**per serve** 21.8g fat; 3045kJ

**serving suggestion** Serve with a salad of baby rocket leaves drizzled with balsamic vinegar.

**tip** Freeze ravioli in single layers between sheets of plastic wrap to make it easier to thaw only a particular amount.

*Roasting tomatoes and onions*

*Cooking ravioli in boiling water*

# lamb and rosemary pie

**2kg boned lamb shoulder**
**2 tablespoons olive oil**
**4 medium brown onions (600g), chopped coarsely**
**2 cloves garlic, crushed**
**1/2 cup plain flour (75g)**
**1/2 cup tomato paste (135g)**
**1 litre beef stock (4 cups)**
**2 tablespoons Worcestershire sauce**
**1 tablespoon finely chopped fresh rosemary**
**1 egg, beaten lightly**
**2 sheets ready-rolled puff pastry**

1 Trim excess fat from lamb; cut lamb into 2cm pieces.

2 Heat oil in large heavy-base saucepan; cook lamb, in batches, until browned all over. Add onion and garlic to same pan; cook, stirring, until onion is soft. Add flour and paste; cook, stirring, until mixture thickens and bubbles. Gradually stir in stock and sauce; stir until mixture boils and thickens.

3 Return lamb (and any juices) to pan; simmer, uncovered, about 45 minutes or until lamb is tender. Stir in rosemary. *[Can be frozen as is, covered, at this stage.]*

4 Preheat oven to hot. Place cooled lamb mixture into two 1.5-litre (6-cup) ovenproof dishes. Brush around edge of each dish with egg; top each with 1 of the sheets of pastry, gently press to seal, trim edges. *[One or both pies can be frozen, covered, at this stage.]*

5 Brush pies with remaining egg; bake, uncovered, in hot oven about 20 minutes. Cover loosely with foil if necessary to prevent overbrowning; bake in hot oven about 25 minutes or until pastry is well browned.

SERVES 8

**per serve** 24g fat; 2337kJ

**serving suggestion** Serve with steamed sugar snap peas, finger zucchini and baby carrots.

**tip** Decorate tops of pies with pastry offcuts, if desired.

*Adding tomato paste and flour to pan*

*Trimming pastry with a knife*

# madras lamb curry with roti

*Roti, sometimes known as chapati, is an unleavened flat bread used in place of cutlery to pick up wet curries when eating an Indian meal. The besan (also called gram flour) used in the recipe is flour made from ground dried chickpeas and is readily available from both Indian and health food stores.*

2 tablespoons peanut oil
1.5kg diced lamb
2 medium brown onions (300g), chopped coarsely
2 cloves garlic, crushed
1 tablespoon ground cumin
2 tablespoons ground coriander
2 teaspoons garam masala
1 teaspoon chilli powder
1 cinnamon stick
5 medium tomatoes (1kg), chopped coarsely
3 cups beef stock (750ml)
400ml coconut cream

ROTI

1¹/2 cups besan (225g)
1¹/2 cups wholemeal plain flour (240g)
1¹/2 cups plain flour (225g)
1¹/2 teaspoons salt
80g ghee
2 tablespoons finely chopped fresh coriander leaves
1 cup warm water (250ml), approximately

1 Heat half of the oil in large heavy-base saucepan; cook lamb, in batches, until browned all over.

2 Heat remaining oil in same pan; cook onion and garlic, stirring, until onion is soft. Add spices, chilli and cinnamon; cook, stirring, about 2 minutes or until fragrant.

3 Return lamb to pan with tomato and stock, bring to boil; simmer, uncovered, 1¹/2 hours. *[Can be frozen, as is or in portions, covered, at this stage.]*

4 Add coconut cream; simmer, uncovered, about 10 minutes or until sauce is just thickened. Serve curry with roti.

**roti** Sift flours and salt into large bowl; rub in ghee. Stir in coriander and just enough of the water to form a soft dough. Knead on floured surface about 5 minutes or until dough is smooth and elastic. Divide dough into 16 pieces; roll each piece into a 17cm-round roti. Stack roti between pieces of plastic wrap then cover completely with plastic wrap to avoid roti drying out. *[Can be frozen, as is or in portions, at this stage.]* Cook roti, in batches, on heated oiled grill plate (or grill or barbecue) until browned both sides and slightly puffed.

SERVES 8

**per serve**  37.4g fat; 3289kJ

**serving suggestion**  Complement this dish with a dry vegetable curry of cauliflower, potato and peas.

**tip**  Pass each roti over a naked flame just before serving to make it puff and become more supple.

*Rolling dough into 17cm rounds*

*Browning lamb in batches*

# lamb souvlakia

*For this recipe, soak 16 bamboo skewers in cold water for at least an hour to avoid them splintering or scorching.*

**1.5kg boned lamb shoulder**
**1/4 cup olive oil (60ml)**
**2 teaspoons finely grated lemon rind**
**1/2 cup lemon juice (125ml)**
**2 cloves garlic, crushed**
**2 tablespoons finely chopped fresh oregano leaves**
**400ml yogurt**
**2 Lebanese cucumbers (260g), seeded, chopped finely**
**2 cloves garlic, crushed, extra**
**8 large pitta**
**4 medium tomatoes (760g), sliced thinly**

1  Trim fat from lamb; cut lamb into 3cm pieces. Combine lamb in large bowl with oil, rind, juice, garlic and oregano. Cover; refrigerate 3 hours or overnight. *[Can be frozen as is, covered, at this stage.]*

2  Meanwhile, combine yogurt, cucumber and extra garlic in small bowl. Cover; refrigerate 3 hours or overnight.

3  Thread meat evenly on skewers; cook, in batches, on heated oiled grill plate (or grill or barbecue) until browned all over and cooked as desired. Serve souvlakia with cucumber yogurt, pitta and tomato.

SERVES 8

**per serve**  17.4g fat; 2257kJ

**serving suggestion**  Serve this delicious dish with a pistachio pilaf.

**tip**  Lamb can be threaded onto skewers then frozen with the marinade, if desired. Freeze skewers in marinade, in batches of four, in freezer bags. Seal bags with pointed ends of skewers protruding from the top to avoid them piercing the bags.

*Trimming fat from the lamb*

*Pulling oregano leaves off stems*

74

# curried lamb shanks with naan

16 frenched lamb shanks
1/4 cup plain flour (35g)
60g ghee
2 large brown onions (400g),
    chopped coarsely
3 cloves garlic, crushed
2 tablespoons grated fresh ginger
2 cinnamon sticks
6 cardamom pods, bruised
1/2 teaspoon ground turmeric
1 tablespoon ground coriander
1/2 cup unsalted roasted cashews
    (75g), chopped finely
3/4 cup water (180ml)
3 cups beef stock (750ml)
2 x 400g cans tomatoes
2 teaspoons sugar
1/4 cup coconut milk (60ml)
1/4 cup coarsely chopped fresh
    coriander leaves

NAAN

1 cup warm water (250ml)
1 teaspoon dry yeast
1 1/2 teaspoons sugar
3 cups plain flour (450g)
1 teaspoon salt
1/4 cup yogurt (60ml)
125g ghee, melted
1 tablespoon black onion seeds

1 Toss lamb in flour, shaking away excess. Heat half of the ghee in large heavy-base saucepan; cook lamb, in batches, until browned all over.

2 Heat remaining ghee in same pan; cook onion, garlic and ginger, stirring, until onion is soft. Add spices and nuts; cook, stirring, until fragrant.

3 Return lamb to pan with the water, stock, undrained crushed tomatoes and sugar; bring to a boil. Simmer, covered, about 1 1/2 hours or until lamb is tender. *[Can be frozen as is, covered, at this stage.]*

4 Add coconut milk; simmer, uncovered, about 20 minutes or until sauce is just thickened. Just before serving, stir in coriander. Serve lamb shank curry with naan.

**naan** Whisk the water with yeast and sugar in small bowl until yeast dissolves, cover; stand in warm place 10 minutes. Sift flour and salt into large bowl; add yeast mixture, yogurt and half of the ghee, mix to a soft dough. Knead on floured surface about 5 minutes or until dough is smooth and elastic. Place dough in large oiled bowl, cover; stand in warm place about 1 1/2 hours or until the dough has doubled in size. Punch down dough; knead on a floured surface 5 minutes. Divide dough into 8 pieces; roll each piece into a 20cm round. Line oven tray with foil; grease foil with a little of the remaining ghee. Cook naan, one at a time, under very hot grill about 2 minutes each side or until puffed and just browned. Brush one side with a little of the remaining ghee, sprinkle with seeds; grill naan 30 seconds. Keep naan warm while cooking remainder. *[Can be frozen, as is or in portions, covered, at this stage.]*

SERVES 8

**per serve** 34.8g fat; 3209kJ

**serving suggestion** Serve with channa dhal or a mixed vegetable curry.

tip You can buy packages of naan bread-mix from supermarkets rather than making your own from scratch.

*Browning lamb shanks all over*

*Punching down the doubled-in-size dough*

# pork

Because so many pork casseroles and stews call for long or slow cooking, they are ideal to be made whenever time isn't the issue but fullness of flavour is: perfect dishes to be frozen.

## flemish pork

*Browning whole baby onions*

*Cooking flour with pork and onions*

**¹/₄ cup olive oil (60ml)**
**1kg baby onions**
**2kg diced pork**
**¹/₃ cup plain flour (50g)**
**1.75 litres vegetable stock (7 cups)**
**3 cups beer (750ml)**
**²/₃ cup cider vinegar (160ml)**
**800g baby carrots, trimmed**
**1kg tiny new potatoes**
**2 tablespoons coarsely chopped fresh flat-leaf parsley**

1  Heat half the oil in large saucepan; cook onions, stirring, until browned, remove from pan. Heat remaining oil in same pan; cook pork, in batches, until browned all over.

2  Return onions and pork to pan with flour; cook, stirring, 2 minutes. Stir in stock, beer and vinegar; bring to boil. Simmer, uncovered, about 1¹/₂ hours or until pork is tender and liquid reduced by half. *[Can be frozen, as is or in portions, covered, at this stage.]*

3  Meanwhile, boil, steam or microwave carrots and potatoes, separately, until just tender; drain.

4  Add vegetables to pork mixture; simmer, uncovered, about 10 minutes or until hot. Just before serving, stir in parsley.

SERVES 8

**per serve**  40.2g fat; 3328kJ

**serving suggestion**  Serve with fresh rye bread and apple sauce.

**tip**  If not freezing this dish, add carrots and potatoes after first 45 minutes of cooking time.

# cassoulet of sausage and chicken

**500g dried haricot beans**
**6 chicken drummettes (400g)**
**1/4 cup olive oil (60ml)**
**750g thick pork sausages**
**2 medium brown onions (300g),**
  **chopped finely**
**4 cloves garlic, crushed**
**2 trimmed celery sticks (150g),**
  **chopped finely**
**1 medium carrot (120g),**
  **chopped finely**
**4 bacon rashers, chopped finely**
**2 x 440g cans tomatoes**
**1¹/₂ cups chicken stock (375ml)**
**2 tablespoons finely chopped**
  **fresh sage leaves**
**6 black peppercorns**
**2 bay leaves**
**2 cups stale breadcrumbs (140g)**

1 Place beans in large bowl, cover with water; soak overnight, drain.

2 Place beans in large saucepan of boiling water; cook, uncovered, until beans are just tender, drain.

3 Meanwhile, remove and discard skin from chicken. Heat half of the oil in large flameproof baking dish; cook sausages and chicken, in batches, until browned. Drain on absorbent paper; slice sausages thickly. Wipe pan clean with absorbent paper.

4 Preheat oven to moderately slow. Heat remaining oil in same pan; cook onion, garlic, celery, carrot and bacon, stirring, about 10 minutes or until browned. Add undrained crushed tomatoes, stock, sage, peppercorns and bay leaves; bring to a boil. Stir in beans, sausages and chicken; sprinkle over breadcrumbs.

5 Bake, uncovered, in moderately slow oven about 2 hours or until crust is browned and meat cooked. It may be necessary to add extra stock when reheating frozen portion if cassoulet thickens too much – you can also stir in an equivalent amount of water. *[Can be frozen, as is or in portions, covered, at this stage.]*

SERVES 8

**per serve** 38g fat; 2830kJ

**serving suggestion** Serve with a French baguette and a mixed leaf salad.

tip Prepare the cassoulet to the end of step 3 but do not top with breadcrumbs. Divide the mixture between two baking dishes, then sprinkle even amounts of breadcrumbs over the cassoulet in each dish; bake one dish now. Freeze the second, covered, unbaked; bake, after thawing overnight in the refrigerator, as explained in step 4.

*Draining haricot beans*

*Sprinkling breadcrumbs over cassoulet*

# hungarian cabbage rolls

*Cutting ribs out of cabbage leaf*

*Rolling cabbage, folding in sides of each leaf*

*You need 16 large cabbage leaves for this recipe. Cabbage rolls are best frozen uncooked; frozen cooked cabbage rolls can be bitter tasting.*

**1 medium Savoy cabbage (1.5kg)**
**1 tablespoon olive oil**
**2 medium brown onions (300g), chopped finely**
**2 cloves garlic, crushed**
**4 trimmed celery sticks (300g), chopped finely**
**2 bacon rashers, chopped finely**
**700g minced pork**
**1 cup long-grain white rice (200g)**
**¹/₃ cup tomato paste (80g)**
**400g can tomatoes**
**3 cups chicken stock (750ml)**
**2 bay leaves**

1 Using a sharp knife, cut out core from bottom of cabbage. Add whole cabbage to large saucepan of boiling water; cook, uncovered, about 7 minutes, turning occasionally, or until leaves just soften. Place cabbage, core-side down, in colander, drain. Carefully pull off 16 large leaves without tearing; trim and discard the hard centre ribs from each leaf. Place leaves flat on absorbent paper to dry.

2 Heat oil in large saucepan; cook onion and garlic, stirring, until onion is soft. Add celery and bacon; cook, stirring, until celery is tender and bacon cooked through. Add pork; cook, stirring, until browned. Remove from heat; stir in rice and 1 tablespoon of the paste.

3 Place ¹/₃-cup of the pork mixture in centre of each cabbage leaf, vein-side up; fold in sides, roll to enclose filling. *[Can be frozen, as is or in portions, covered, at this stage.]*

4 Preheat oven to moderate. Combine undrained crushed tomatoes, remaining paste, stock and bay leaves in large bowl. *[Can be frozen, as is or in portions, covered, at this stage.]*

5 Place rolls, seam-side down, in single layer in large baking dish. Pour tomato mixture over rolls; cook, covered, in moderate oven about 1 hour or until rice is tender and rolls cooked through. Discard bay leaves before serving.

SERVES 8

**per serve**  5.6g fat; 1244kJ

**serving suggestion**  Top cabbage rolls with a tablespoon of sour cream and a sprinkling of sweet paprika; accompany with fresh crusty bread.

# auntie rose's pasta sauce

**8 chicken wings (680g)**
**1 tablespoon olive oil**
**8 pork loin chops (2.25kg)**
**1 medium brown onion (150g), chopped finely**
**2 cloves garlic, crushed**
**2 tablespoons brandy**
**600g jar tomato pasta sauce**
**2 cups tomato paste (500g)**
**1.5 litres water (6 cups)**
**1/4 cup finely shredded fresh basil leaves**

1 Cut chicken wings into three pieces at the joints; discard wing tip.

2 Heat oil in large heavy-base saucepan; cook chicken and pork, in batches, until browned all over.

3 Cook onion and garlic in same pan, stirring, until onion is soft. Add brandy; cook, stirring, until liquid has evaporated by half. Stir in pasta sauce, paste and the water.

4 Return chicken and pork to pan; bring mixture to boil. Simmer, uncovered, about 2 hours or until chicken and pork are cooked through and very tender. *[Can be frozen, as is or in portions, covered, at this stage.]* Just before serving, stir in basil.

SERVES 8

**per serve** 30g fat; 2203kJ

**serving suggestion** This sauce is good with penne – it's hollow and thus captures the sauce.

**tip** When cooked, the meat should be so tender it is literally falling off the bone, almost in shreds.

*Cutting chicken wings*

*Adding chicken and pork to sauce*

# wonton and vegetable soup

*Ask your butcher or chicken shop to save the chicken bones for you; they are often available, already packaged, for making stock. Frozen wontons do not need to be thawed before being cooked in the soup.*

**2 medium brown onions (300g), chopped coarsely**
**2 medium carrots (240g), chopped coarsely**
**2 trimmed celery sticks (150g), chopped coarsely**
**1.5kg chicken bones**
**8 black peppercorns**
**2 bay leaves**
**3 litres water (12 cups)**
**1/3 cup soy sauce (80ml)**
**1 tablespoon peanut oil**
**1 medium brown onion (150g), chopped finely, extra**
**2 teaspoons grated fresh ginger**
**1 clove garlic, crushed**
**400g minced pork**
**1 tablespoon oyster sauce**
**40 wonton wrappers**
**1 egg, beaten lightly**
**300g Chinese water spinach, trimmed, chopped coarsely**
**4 green onions, sliced thinly**

1 Combine brown onion, carrot, celery, chicken bones, peppercorns, bay leaves and the water in large saucepan, bring to boil; simmer, uncovered, 2 hours.

2 Strain chicken mixture through muslin-lined sieve over large bowl. Discard solids; reserve stock. Return stock to same pan, stir in half of the soy sauce, bring to boil; simmer, uncovered, 10 minutes. *[Best made ahead to this stage. Cover; freeze or refrigerate overnight.]*

3 Heat oil in medium saucepan; cook extra brown onion, ginger and garlic, stirring, until onion is soft. Remove from heat; stir in pork, remaining soy sauce and oyster sauce in medium bowl.

4 Place a rounded teaspoon of the pork mixture in centre of each wrapper; brush edges with egg, pinch edges together to seal. Repeat with remaining wrappers, pork mixture and egg. Place wontons, in single layer, on tray. *[Can be frozen, as is or in portions, covered, at this stage.]*

5 Add wontons to simmering stock; simmer, uncovered, about 10 minutes or until wontons are cooked through. Just before serving, stir water spinach and green onion into soup.

SERVES 8

**per serve**  4.9g fat; 956kJ

**serving suggestions**  Makes a light lunch when served with a few deep-fried spring rolls and a bowl of steamed rice.

*Trimming water spinach from stalks*

*Pinching together edges of filled wontons*

# baked chorizo and polenta

*Stirring polenta until it thickens slightly*

*Layering chorizo slices over polenta*

*Chorizo is a spicy Spanish sausage made from pork, garlic and red peppers.*

**1 tablespoon olive oil**
**2 medium brown onions (300g), chopped finely**
**4 cloves garlic, crushed**
**3 x 400g cans tomatoes**
**1/2 cup tomato paste (125g)**
**2 tablespoons coarsely chopped fresh basil leaves**
**1kg chorizo sausages**
**1 litre vegetable stock (4 cups)**
**2 1/2 cups milk (625ml)**
**2 cups polenta (340g)**
**1 cup finely grated parmesan cheese (80g)**
**50g butter**
**300g mozzarella cheese, sliced thinly**

1 Heat oil in large saucepan; cook onion and garlic, stirring, until onion is soft. Add undrained crushed tomatoes and paste; bring to boil. Simmer, uncovered, about 15 minutes or until thickened slightly; stir in basil. *[Can be frozen, as is or in portions, covered, at this stage.]*

2 Cook chorizo, in batches, in medium heated dry frying pan, until browned all over; drain on absorbent paper. Slice chorizo coarsely.

3 Preheat oven to hot. Oil two 2-litre (8-cup) shallow baking dishes.

4 Bring combined stock and milk to boil in large saucepan; gradually stir in polenta. Simmer, stirring, about 5 minutes or until polenta thickens slightly. Stir in parmesan and butter.

5 Divide polenta between prepared dishes; smoothing with a palette knife. Top each with chorizo then tomato sauce. *[Can be frozen, as is or in portions, covered, at this stage.]*

6 Bake, covered, in hot oven 30 minutes. Top with mozzarella; bake, uncovered, about 10 minutes or until cheese melts and browns slightly.

SERVES 8

**per serve** 61.2g fat; 4010kJ

**serving suggestion** Homemade guacamole and corn chips make great accompaniments to this dish.

**tip** If chorizo is unavailable, use any spicy thick pork sausage, draining away all the fat after it has been browned.

# seafood

Did you go overboard at the fish markets on the weekend?
Turn the surplus into these surprisingly simple main courses then, later
in the week, open your freezer for what really is the catch of the day!

# herbed swordfish kebabs

*You need 16 bamboo skewers for this recipe; remember to soak them in water for an hour or so before using to avoid them splintering or scorching.*

**2kg swordfish steaks**
**4 medium lemons (560g)**
**1/3 cup finely chopped fresh**
   **coriander leaves**
**1/2 cup finely chopped fresh**
   **flat-leaf parsley**
**1/2 cup finely chopped**
   **fresh chives**
**1/2 teaspoon cracked black pepper**
**2 tablespoons peanut oil**

1 Remove and discard skin from fish; cut into 3cm pieces.

2 Using citrus zester, remove as much rind as possible from the lemons. Squeeze only as many of the lemons as needed to make 2/3 cup juice (160ml); remaining lemons will keep, under refrigeration, up to 1 week.

3 Combine fish in large bowl with rind, juice, herbs, pepper and oil; toss to mix well.

4 Thread fish onto 16 skewers; place, in single layer, in large shallow dish. Pour any remaining marinade in bowl over skewers, cover; refrigerate 2 hours or overnight. *[Can be frozen, covered, in 4-skewer portions, at this stage.]* Cook skewers on heated oiled grill plate (or grill or barbecue) until browned all over and cooked through.

SERVES 8

**per serve** 11.8g fat; 1346kJ

**serving suggestion** Serve with baby spinach leaves tossed in a lemon vinaigrette.

**tips** The fish is frozen already skewered because it can be difficult to thread after thawing.

• Squeeze all the lemons and freeze the extra juice in ice block trays.

*Cutting fish into even-size cubes*

*Zesting the lemon rind*

# prawn and crab wontons

Combining prawns and other ingredients

Pinching wonton edges to seal

*Frozen wontons can be deep-fried as is; freeze 8-wonton portions so you can take only as many as you need.*

**500g uncooked prawns**
**500g crabmeat**
**1 teaspoon grated fresh ginger**
**1 clove garlic, crushed**
**4 green onions, chopped finely**
**1 tablespoon soy sauce**
**1 tablespoon sweet chilli sauce**
**80 wonton wrappers**
**1 tablespoon cornflour**
**1 tablespoon water**
**peanut oil, for deep-frying**

DIPPING SAUCE

**2 teaspoons soy sauce**
**2 tablespoons sweet chilli sauce**
**1 teaspoon dry sherry**
**1 green onion, chopped finely**

1   Shell and devein prawns; chop prawn meat finely.

2   Combine prawn meat in medium bowl with crab, ginger, garlic, onion and sauces.

3   Place 1 heaped teaspoon of prawn mixture in centre of each wrapper; brush edges with blended cornflour and water, pinch edges together to seal. Repeat with remaining wrappers, prawn mixture and cornflour paste. *[Can be frozen, as is or in portions, covered, at this stage.]*

4   Heat oil in large deep-frying pan; deep-fry wontons, in batches, until browned and cooked through. Drain on absorbent paper; serve with dipping sauce.

**dipping sauce**   Combine ingredients in small bowl.

SERVES 8 (MAKES 80)

**per serve**   8.6g fat; 3480kJ

**serving suggestion**   These wontons are good as finger food to serve with cocktails.

tip   Canned crabmeat can be used; drain well.

# thai fish cakes

*We used fresh ling fillets, but you can use any firm white fish you like in this recipe.*

**2kg white fish fillets**
**1/3 cup finely chopped fresh lemon grass**
**12 kaffir lime leaves, shredded**
**2 tablespoons grated fresh ginger**
**2 red Thai chillies, seeded, chopped finely**
**1/3 cup finely chopped fresh coriander leaves**
**2/3 cup water (160ml)**
**1/3 cup lime juice (80ml)**
**1/2 cup caster sugar (110g)**
**1 green Thai chilli, seeded, chopped finely**
**1 small cucumber (130g), seeded, chopped finely**

1 Discard any skin and bones from fish; blend or process fish until a smooth paste forms.

2 Combine fish in large bowl with lemon grass, lime leaves, ginger, red chilli and coriander.

3 Divide fish mixture into 16 equal parts. Using hands, shape each part into a patty; place on tray, repeat process with remaining mixture. Cover; refrigerate 30 minutes. *[Can be frozen, as is or in portions, covered, at this stage.]*

4 Heat the water, juice and sugar in small saucepan; cook, stirring, over heat until sugar is dissolved. Bring to a boil; cool. Add chilli and cucumber.

5 Cook fish cakes in heated oiled large frying pan, in batches, until browned both sides and cooked through. Serve fish cakes with dipping sauce.

SERVES 8 (MAKES 16)

**per serve** 7.1g fat; 1382kJ

**serving suggestion** Serve with a vegetarian version of pad thai, with tofu added in place of seafood.

**tip** Sugar syrup will keep 2 days, covered, in the refrigerator.

*Seeding the chillies helps reduce their heat*

*Combining fish with other ingredients*

# octopus in red wine

**2kg baby octopus**
**2 tablespoons olive oil**
**1 large red onion (200g), chopped finely**
**2 cloves garlic, crushed**
**3/4 cup dry red wine (180ml)**
**2 x 400g cans tomatoes**
**1/2 cup water (125ml)**
**1/3 cup torn fresh basil leaves**
**100g kalamata olives, seeded**
**1 tablespoon drained capers, chopped finely**

1 Cut heads from octopus just below eyes, discard heads; remove beaks. Wash octopus.

2 Place octopus in heated dry large saucepan; simmer, covered, 15 minutes. Drain octopus; discard pan liquid. Wipe pan with absorbent paper.

3 Heat oil in same pan; cook onion, stirring, until soft. Add garlic and octopus; cook, stirring, 5 minutes. Add wine; cook, stirring, until most of the liquid has evaporated. Add undrained crushed tomatoes and the water; simmer, covered, about 1 1/2 hours or until octopus is tender. *[Can be frozen, as is or in portions, covered, at this stage.]* Just before serving, stir in basil, olives and capers.

SERVES 8

**per serve** 13.7g fat; 1147kJ

**serving suggestion** Serve with rocket leaves sprinkled with balsamic vinegar, and a fresh loaf of wood-fired bread.

tip Buy the octopus already cleaned and cut up, if possible.

*Preparing the octopus*

*Crushing canned tomatoes with scissors*

# vegetarian

The humble veg is all too often forgotten in the rush, but the enticing selection in this chapter will have you pushing these bit players onto centre stage – out of the freezer straight into the limelight!

## mixed dhal

*Combining seeds, spices and onion mixture*

*Adding lentils, beans and peas to pan*

**60g ghee**
**2 medium brown onions (300g), chopped finely**
**2 cloves garlic, crushed**
**1 tablespoon grated fresh ginger**
**1¹/₂ tablespoons black mustard seeds**
**1¹/₂ tablespoons ground cumin**
**1¹/₂ tablespoons ground coriander**
**2 teaspoons ground turmeric**
**³/₄ cup brown lentils (150g)**
**³/₄ cup red lentils (150g)**
**³/₄ cup yellow mung beans (150g)**
**³/₄ cup green split peas (150g)**
**2 x 400g cans tomatoes**
**1 litre vegetable stock (4 cups)**
**²/₃ cup coconut cream (160ml)**
**¹/₄ cup coarsely chopped fresh coriander leaves**

1   Heat ghee in large heavy-base saucepan; cook onion, garlic and ginger, stirring, until onion is soft. Add seeds and spices; cook, stirring, until fragrant.

2   Add lentils, beans and peas to pan; stir to combine. Add undrained crushed tomatoes and stock; bring to a boil. Simmer, covered, about 1 hour, stirring occasionally, until lentils are tender and mixture thickens. *[Can be frozen, as is or in portions, covered, at this stage.]*

3   Just before serving, add coconut cream and coriander; stir over low heat until dhal is heated through.

SERVES 8

**per serve**   14.3g fat; 1565kJ

**serving suggestion**   Serve with basmati rice or spinach pilaf, and homemade roti.

tip   Clarify ordinary butter if ghee is unavailable by heating butter in small pan until white sediment comes to the surface; skim and discard sediment, use the remaining heavy "oil".

# caramelised onion tart

3 cups plain flour (450g)
250g butter, chopped
2 egg yolks
1/4 cup cold water (60ml)
50g butter, extra
2 large brown onions (400g),
  sliced thinly
2 cloves garlic, crushed
2 tablespoons brown sugar
1 1/2 tablespoons balsamic vinegar
1/4 cup chicken stock (60ml)
12 eggs, beaten lightly
3/4 cup cream (180ml)

TRADITIONAL PESTO

1 clove garlic, quartered
1 cup firmly packed fresh
  basil leaves
1/4 cup pine nuts (40g), toasted
1/2 cup coarsely grated
  parmesan cheese (40g)
1/4 cup light olive oil (60ml)

1  Process flour and butter until crumbly; add egg yolks and the water, process until ingredients just come together. Knead mixture gently on floured surface until smooth, wrap in plastic wrap; refrigerate dough 30 minutes.

2  Oil two 22cm loose-base flan tins. Roll half the pastry between sheets of baking paper until large enough to line base and side of one prepared tin. Lift pastry into tin, ease into side; trim edges. Repeat with remaining tin and pastry. Cover each tin with plastic wrap; refrigerate 30 minutes.

3  Preheat oven to moderately hot. Discard plastic wrap covering tins; place a sheet of baking paper in tin on pastry, fill with dried beans or rice. Place tins on oven trays; bake, uncovered, in moderately hot oven 10 minutes. Remove beans and paper, return tins to oven; bake, uncovered, about 10 minutes or until tart cases are browned evenly.

4  Meanwhile, melt extra butter in large frying pan; cook onion and garlic, stirring, until onion is soft. Add sugar, vinegar and stock; cook, stirring, about 15 minutes or until onion caramelises and liquid evaporates, cool.

5  Reduce oven to moderately slow. Divide onion mixture between tart cases; pour combined eggs and cream evenly over onion mixture.

6  Bake, uncovered, in moderately slow oven about 20 minutes or until filling is set. Serve tarts, hot or cooled, with pesto. *[Can be made ahead to this stage. Cover; refrigerate overnight or freeze, covered separately, as is.]*

**traditional pesto**  Blend or process garlic, basil, nuts and parmesan until combined. With motor operating, gradually pour in oil; process until a thick paste forms. *[Can be made ahead to this stage. Cover; refrigerate overnight or freeze, covered, in two portions.]*

SERVES 8

**per serve**  74.2g fat; 3889kJ

**serving suggestion**  Serve with a salad of bitter greens with a classic lemon vinaigrette.

**tip**  Baby spinach leaves and chopped roasted tomatoes can replace the onion for another vegetarian variation.

*Blind-baking tart cases*

*Pouring egg and cream mixture into tart case*

# lentil and spinach soup

**2 tablespoons peanut oil**
**2 large brown onions (400g), chopped finely**
**2 cloves garlic, crushed**
**2 teaspoons ground cumin**
**1 teaspoon ground turmeric**
**1 teaspoon ground coriander**
**3 cups red lentils (600g)**
**1.25 litres vegetable stock (5 cups)**
**1 litre water (4 cups)**
**500g spinach, trimmed, chopped finely**

1 Heat oil in large saucepan; cook onion and garlic, stirring, until onion is soft. Add spices; cook, stirring, until fragrant.

2 Add lentils; stir to combine with spice mixture. Add stock and water; bring to a boil. Simmer soup, uncovered, about 25 minutes, or until lentils are tender.

3 Blend or process soup, in batches, until smooth. *[Can be frozen, as is or in portions, covered, at this stage.]* Return soup to pan, add spinach; stir over heat until hot.

SERVES 8

**per serve** 6.8g fat; 1174kJ

**serving suggestion** Serve as an entree for an Indian meal.

**tips** Soup can be thinned with a little stock or water when it is thawed, if necessary.

• If you own a hand-held stab mixer, you can process the soup in the pan it's cooked in.

*Coating lentils in spice mixture*

*Adding finely chopped spinach to soup*

# pumpkin gnocchi with rocket pesto

*You will need about 1.25kg of unpeeled pumpkin for this recipe. If freezing only half of the gnocchi, freeze the same proportion of the pesto. Likewise, if you plan on serving half the gnocchi at a time, heat only 300ml of cream with 1 tablespoon of the pesto. Gnocchi can be cooked straight from the freezer.*

**1 cup firmly packed fresh
   baby rocket leaves
1/2 cup pistachios (90g), toasted
2 cloves garlic, quartered
1/2 cup coarsely grated
   parmesan cheese (40g)
1/4 cup olive oil (60ml)
800g coarsely chopped pumpkin
1 tablespoon olive oil, extra
2 large potatoes (600g),
   chopped coarsely
1 egg, beaten lightly
1 egg yolk
2 cups plain flour (300g)
600ml cream**

1 Blend or process rocket, nuts, garlic and cheese until chopped coarsely. With motor operating, gradually pour in oil; process until a thick paste forms. *[Can be made ahead to this stage. Cover; refrigerate pesto overnight, or freeze, covered, as is or in portions.]*

2 Preheat oven to hot. Toss pumpkin with extra oil in large baking dish; bake, uncovered, in hot oven about 45 minutes or until pumpkin is tender. Boil, steam or microwave potato until tender; drain.

3 Mash pumpkin and potato in large bowl until smooth; stir in egg and egg yolk. Using floured hand, mix in flour. Turn pumpkin mixture onto floured surface; knead about 2 minutes or until smooth.

4 Using floured hands, roll heaped teaspoons of pumpkin mixture into gnocchi-shaped ovals. Place each oval in palm of hand; press with inverted floured fork tines to flatten gnocchi slightly and make grooved imprint. Repeat with remaining pumpkin mixture. *[Can be made ahead to this stage. Cover; refrigerate gnocchi overnight, or freeze, covered, as is or in portions.]*

5 Just before serving, place gnocchi into large pan of boiling water; cook, uncovered, about 3 minutes or until gnocchi float to surface. Remove from pan with slotted spoon; drain.

6 Working quickly, while gnocchi are cooking, heat cream with 2 tablespoons of the pesto in medium saucepan. Pour over drained gnocchi; toss gently to combine. Serve topped with additional pesto to taste.

SERVES 8

**per serve** 51.3g fat; 2943kJ
**serving suggestion** Serve with fresh wood-fired bread and a simple tomato and basil salad.
**tip** Freeze cooked cooled gnocchi, in a single layer, on tray; cover tightly with plastic wrap.

*Making indentations in gnocchi with fork tines*

*Cooked gnocchi floating to surface of water*

# spanakopita

*For this recipe, use silverbeet, also known as Swiss chard, rather than spinach.*

**1.5kg silverbeet, trimmed**
**1 tablespoon olive oil**
**1 medium brown onion (150g), chopped finely**
**2 cloves garlic, crushed**
**1 teaspoon ground nutmeg**
**200g fetta, crumbled**
**1 tablespoon finely grated lemon rind**
**¼ cup coarsely chopped fresh mint leaves**
**¼ cup coarsely chopped fresh flat-leaf parsley**
**¼ cup coarsely chopped fresh dill**
**4 green onions, chopped finely**
**16 sheets fillo pastry**
**125g butter, melted**
**2 teaspoons sesame seeds**

1 Boil, steam or microwave silverbeet until just wilted; drain. Squeeze out excess moisture; drain on absorbent paper. Chop silverbeet coarsely; spread out on absorbent paper.

2 Heat oil in small frying pan; cook brown onion and garlic, stirring, until onion is soft. Add nutmeg; cook, stirring, until fragrant. Combine onion mixture and silverbeet in large bowl with fetta, rind, herbs and green onion. *[Can be made ahead to this stage. Cover; refrigerate overnight.]*

3 Brush 1 sheet of the fillo with butter; fold lengthways into thirds, brushing with butter between each fold. Place rounded tablespoons of the silverbeet mixture at bottom of one narrow edge of folded fillo sheet, leaving a border. Fold opposite corner of fillo diagonally across the filling to form large triangle; continue folding to end of fillo sheet, retaining triangular shape. Place on lightly oiled oven trays, seam-side down; repeat with remaining ingredients until 16 spanakopita are made. *[Can be frozen, in groups of 4, covered, at this stage.]*

4 Preheat oven to moderate. Brush spanakopita with remaining butter; sprinkle with sesame seeds. Bake, uncovered, in moderate oven about 15 minutes or until browned lightly.

SERVES 8

**per serve** 23.2g fat; 1330kJ

**serving suggestion** Drizzle a mixture of chopped cucumber and yogurt over the top of the spanakopitas.

**tip** To prevent fillo drying out, keep it covered with damp tea-towel until ready to use.

*Folding each sheet of fillo into thirds*

*Making triangles with filled fillo*

# carrot soup with buttermilk damper

2 tablespoons peanut oil
4 medium brown onions (600g),
   chopped coarsely
2 cloves garlic, quartered
2 tablespoons grated fresh ginger
8 kaffir lime leaves, torn
1 tablespoon ground cumin
1 tablespoon ground coriander
2kg carrots, chopped coarsely
1.5 litres vegetable stock (6 cups)
2 litres water (8 cups)
2 large potatoes (600g),
   chopped coarsely
2 cups coconut cream (500ml)
2 tablespoons coarsely chopped
   fresh coriander leaves

BUTTERMILK DAMPER

3¹/₂ cups self-raising flour (525g)
40g butter
2 tablespoons sunflower seeds
2 tablespoons linseeds
2 teaspoons poppy seeds
2 teaspoons sesame seeds
2 cups buttermilk (500ml)

1 Heat oil in large heavy-base saucepan; cook onion, garlic, ginger and leaves, stirring, until onion is soft. Add spices; cook, stirring, until fragrant. Add carrot; cook, stirring, 5 minutes.

2 Add stock, the water and potato; bring to a boil. Simmer, uncovered, about 30 minutes or until vegetables are tender.

3 Blend or process soup mixture, in batches, until smooth; return to pan, add coconut cream. *[Can be frozen, as is or in portions, covered, at this stage.]*

4 Bring soup to a boil; simmer, uncovered, about 5 minutes or until hot. Just before serving, stir in coriander; serve with buttermilk damper.

**buttermilk damper** Preheat oven to very hot. Place flour in large bowl; rub in butter. Stir in sunflower seeds, linseeds, half of the poppy seeds, half of the sesame seeds and buttermilk. Turn dough onto floured surface, knead until just smooth; divide dough into eight portions, shape into rounds, place on oiled oven tray. Mark a cross on top of each damper; sprinkle with combined remaining seeds. *[Can be frozen, then individually wrapped in pairs or fours, at this stage.]* Bake, uncovered, in very hot oven about 15 minutes or until dampers sound hollow when tapped. Turn onto wire rack to cool.

SERVES 8

**per serve** 27.9g fat; 2469kJ

**serving suggestion** Serve before a modern take on a traditional curry.

**tip** Substitute the coconut cream with fresh pouring cream, if preferred.

*Cooking carrots, spices and onion mixture*

*Stirring buttermilk into flour mixture*

# vegetable croquettes

*Shaping vegetable mixture into 12cm logs*

*Coating croquettes in breadcrumb mixture*

**2kg potatoes, chopped coarsely**
**1kg pumpkin, chopped coarsely**
**40g butter**
**1 clove garlic, crushed**
**2 green onions, chopped finely**
**2/3 cup frozen peas (80g), thawed, drained**
**2/3 cup finely grated parmesan cheese (50g)**
**1/2 cup plain flour (75g)**
**3 eggs, beaten lightly**
**1 1/2 cups packaged breadcrumbs (150g)**
**2 tablespoons finely chopped fresh flat-leaf parsley**
**vegetable oil, for deep-frying**
**1 cup sour cream (250ml)**
**1/3 cup milk (80ml)**
**1 1/2 tablespoons seeded mustard**
**2 tablespoons finely chopped fresh chives**

1  Boil, steam or microwave potato and pumpkin until very tender; drain. Pass through a food mill (or mash then push through fine sieve) into large bowl.

2  Melt butter in small saucepan; cook garlic and onion, stirring, until onion is soft. Add to bowl with potato mixture; stir in peas and cheese.

3  Using floured hands, roll 1/3 cup of the croquette mixture into 12cm log; coat in flour, shaking away excess. Next, dip croquette in egg then combined breadcrumbs and parsley. Place on tray; continue process until 24 croquettes are made. Cover; refrigerate 30 minutes. *[Can be frozen, as is or in portions, covered, at this stage.]*

4  Heat oil in large saucepan; deep-fry croquettes, in batches, until browned all over and heated through. Drain on absorbent paper; serve with sauce made of combined remaining ingredients.

SERVES 8

**per serve**  39.8g fat; 2836kJ

**serving suggestion**  Vegetable croquettes are the perfect accompaniment to grilled fish or chops.

**tip**  Any leftover roasted vegetables can be mashed for croquettes.

# vegetable curry and paratha

1 tablespoon vegetable oil
2 medium brown onions (300g),
  chopped coarsely
2 cloves garlic, crushed
1 tablespoon black mustard seeds
2 teaspoons cumin seeds
1/2 teaspoon ground turmeric
1 tablespoon ground coriander
1/2 teaspoon ground cinnamon
2 large kumara (1kg),
  chopped coarsely
2 cups vegetable stock (500ml)
400g can tomatoes
2 tablespoons tomato paste
1 1/2 cups coconut milk (375ml)
500g cauliflower, cut into florets
200g green beans, halved
2 x 300g cans chickpeas,
  rinsed, drained
1/4 cup coarsely chopped fresh
  coriander leaves

PARATHA

5 medium potatoes (1kg),
  chopped coarsely
1/2 cup brown lentils (100g)
1 tablespoon vegetable oil
1 medium brown onion (150g),
  chopped coarsely
1 clove garlic, crushed
1 tablespoon black mustard seeds
2 teaspoons garam masala
1/4 cup coarsely chopped fresh
  coriander leaves
3 cups plain wholemeal
  flour (480g)
3 cups plain flour (450g)
2 teaspoons salt
80g butter
2 cups water (500ml),
  approximately

1 Heat oil in large saucepan; cook onion and garlic, stirring, until onion is soft. Add seeds and spices; cook, stirring, until fragrant. Add kumara; cook, stirring, 5 minutes.

2 Add stock, undrained crushed tomatoes and paste; bring to a boil. Simmer, uncovered, about 15 minutes or until kumara is almost tender. Stir in coconut milk and cauliflower; simmer, uncovered, 5 minutes. *[Can be frozen, covered, as is or in portions, at this stage.]*

3 Add beans and chickpeas; simmer, uncovered, about 10 minutes or until vegetables are tender. Just before serving, stir in coriander; serve curry with paratha.

**paratha** Boil, steam or microwave potato until tender, drain; mash until smooth. Cook lentils, uncovered, in small saucepan of boiling water about 15 minutes or until just tender, drain. Heat oil in small frying pan; cook onion and garlic, until onion is soft. Add seeds and garam masala; cook, stirring, until fragrant. Combine onion mixture in large bowl with potato, lentils and coriander. Sift flours and salt into large bowl, rub in butter; add enough of the water to form soft dough. Knead dough on floured surface about 10 minutes or until smooth and elastic, cover with plastic wrap; stand 1 hour. Divide dough into 32 pieces; roll each piece on floured surface into a 14cm-round paratha. Layer paratha as they are rolled, separating each with plastic wrap to prevent their drying out. Spread 16 paratha on floured surface; divide potato filling among them, spreading to within 1cm of the edge. Brush around edges of paratha with a little extra water; top each with one of the remaining paratha, pressing edges together to seal. *[Can be frozen, individually wrapped, at this stage.]* Cook paratha on heated oiled grill plate (or grill or barbecue) until browned both sides and heated through.

SERVES 8

**per serve** 28.7g fat; 3760kJ
**serving suggestion** Accompany this meal with a bowl of cucumber raita.
**tip** The rolled and stacked paratha, and the potato filling, can be covered and frozen separately; thaw, fill and grill the paratha just before serving.

*Cooking spices with onion mixture*

*Enclosing potato filling between paratha*

# lynn's eggplant parmigiana

*Browning eggplant slices by shallow-frying*

*Covering eggplant slices with tomato sauce*

*This delicious eggplant dish is best served on a short fat hollow pasta such as shells.*

**1 medium brown onion (150g), chopped finely**
**2 trimmed celery sticks (150g), chopped finely**
**2 tablespoons brandy**
**2 tablespoons finely chopped fresh flat-leaf parsley**
**3 cups tomato paste (750g)**
**2 litres water (8 cups)**
**1 teaspoon sugar**
**olive oil, for shallow-frying**
**2 large eggplants (1kg), sliced thickly**
**3/4 cup packaged breadcrumbs (75g)**
**1/2 cup grated romano cheese (40g)**
**1kg shell or any short pasta**

1 Heat large heavy-base saucepan; cook onion and celery, stirring, until onion is soft. Add brandy and parsley; cook, stirring, until most of the brandy evaporates. Stir in paste, water and sugar; simmer, uncovered, about 1¼ hours or until sauce thickens slightly.

2 Meanwhile, heat oil in large frying pan; shallow-fry eggplant, in batches, until browned both sides. Drain on absorbent paper.

3 Preheat oven to moderate. Place one-third of the eggplant, in a single layer, in shallow 3-litre (12-cup) ovenproof dish; pour one-third of the tomato sauce over eggplant, sprinkle with half of the breadcrumbs and half of the cheese. Repeat layering process, finishing with eggplant and tomato sauce.

4 Bake eggplant parmigiana, uncovered, in moderate oven about 40 minutes or until almost set. *[Can be frozen, as is or in portions, covered, at this stage.]*

5 Just before serving, cook pasta in large pan of boiling water, uncovered, until just tender; drain. Serve eggplant parmigiana over pasta.

SERVES 8

**per serve** 43.3g fat; 3854kJ

**serving suggestion** Serve with veal schnitzel.

**tip** Eggplant can be sprayed lightly with cooking-oil spray and browned under a grill for a lower-fat version, but browning it by shallow-frying in olive oil is what makes the finished dish so velvety-rich and flavoursome.

# cannellini beans with polenta

*Smoothing polenta mixture flat*

*Cutting the polenta into 16 triangles*

**1 litre water (4 cups)**
**2 cups polenta (340g)**
**1 cup finely grated parmesan cheese (80g)**
**1 tablespoon olive oil**
**1 medium brown onion (150g), sliced thinly**
**1 clove garlic, crushed**
**2 x 400g cans tomatoes**
**3/4 cup vegetable stock (180ml)**
**2 tablespoons tomato paste**
**1 red Thai chilli, seeded, chopped finely**
**2 x 400g cans cannellini beans, rinsed, drained**
**500g spinach, trimmed, chopped coarsely**
**1 tablespoon finely shredded fresh basil leaves**

1 Oil 23cm-square slab pan. Bring the water to a boil in large saucepan. Gradually whisk in polenta; simmer, whisking, about 5 minutes or until mixture thickens. Stir in cheese.

2 Smooth polenta mixture flat in prepared pan, cover; refrigerate about 3 hours or until firm. Turn polenta onto board. Cut polenta in half; cut each half into quarters then each quarter in half diagonally. *[Can be frozen, as is or in portions, covered, at this stage.]*

3 Heat oil in medium saucepan; cook onion and garlic, stirring, until onion is soft. Add undrained crushed tomatoes, stock, paste and chilli; bring to a boil. Simmer tomato mixture, uncovered, about 5 minutes or until thickened slightly.

4 Add beans, spinach and basil; cook, uncovered, until spinach is wilted and beans hot. *[Can be frozen, as is or in portions, covered, at this stage.]*

5 Just before serving, cook polenta triangles, in batches, in dry large heated grill pan until browned both sides; drain on absorbent paper. Serve with tomato and cannellini beans.

SERVES 8

**per serve** 7.4g fat; 1214kJ

**serving suggestion** Serve with mesclun tossed in a balsamic vinaigrette.

**tips** Any kind of dried beans can be soaked overnight, boiled until tender then used, drained, if you prefer not to use canned beans.

• Use patience when spreading polenta into prepared pan: it tends to move and slip but can eventually be worked into the pan's corners.

# glossary

ground cardamom

cardamom seeds

cardamom pods

black cardamom pods

**almond meal** also known as finely ground almonds; powdered to a flour-like texture, used in baking or as a thickening agent.

**bacon rashers** also known as slices of bacon; made from pork side, cured and smoked.

**beetroot** also known as red beets or, simply, beets; firm, round root vegetable. Can be eaten raw, grated, in salads; boiled then sliced; or roasted then mashed like potatoes.

**beans**

BLACK (TURTLE) Latin-American and Caribbean small black bean with a tiny white eye, not to be confused with Chinese black (soy) beans. Sold dried or canned, great in salsas and soups.

BORLOTTI also known as Roman beans; pale pink with darker red spots, eaten fresh or dried.

HARICOT similar in appearance and flavour to other small dried white beans such as great northern, navy and cannellini; sold dried, good in soups and casseroles.

KIDNEY medium-size red bean, slightly floury yet sweet in flavour; sold dried or canned, used in soups, salads and stews.

**bok choy** also called pak choi or Chinese white cabbage; has a fresh, mild mustard taste and is good braised or in stir-fries. Baby bok choy is also available.

**breadcrumbs, stale** One- or two-day-old bread made into crumbs by grating, blending or processing.

**burghul** also known as bulghur wheat; hulled steamed wheat kernels that, once dried, are crushed into various sized grains. Used in Middle-Eastern dishes such as kibbeh and tabbouleh.

curry leaves

**butter** use salted or unsalted ("sweet") butter; 125g is equal to 1 stick butter.

**buttermilk** sold alongside fresh milk products in supermarkets; despite the implication of its name, is low in fat. Commercially made, by a method similar to yogurt. A good low-fat substitution for dairy products such as cream or sour cream; good in baking and in salad dressings.

**capsicum** also known as bell pepper or, simply, pepper. Seeds and membranes should be discarded before use.

**cardamom** native to India and used extensively in its cooking, in pod, seed or pulverised form; one of the world's most expensive spices.

**chicken drummettes** drumsticks (legs) with the end of the bone chopped off; they are sometimes called "lovely legs".

**chillies** available in many types and sizes, both fresh and dried. Use rubber gloves when seeding and chopping fresh chillies as they can burn your skin. Removing seeds and membranes lessens the heat level.

JALAPEÑO sold finely chopped or whole, bottled in vinegar, as well as fresh; we used the medium-hot, sweetish chopped bottled version in our recipes.

SWEET CHILLI SAUCE comparatively mild, Thai-type sauce made from red chillies, sugar, garlic and vinegar.

THAI small, medium hot, and bright-red to dark-green in colour.

**chinese barbecued duck** Traditionally cooked in special ovens, this duck has a sweet-sticky coating made from soy sauce, sherry, five-spice and hoisin sauce. It is available from Asian food stores.

**ciabatta** in Italian, the word means slipper, which is the traditional shape of this popular crisp-crusted white bread.

**coconut**

CREAM the first pressing from grated mature coconut flesh; available in cans and cartons.

MILK the second pressing (less rich) from grated mature coconut flesh; available in cans and cartons. A lower-fat type is also sold.

**coriander** also known as cilantro or Chinese parsley; bright-green-leafed herb with a pungent flavour. Often stirred into a dish just before serving for maximum impact.

**corn**

BABY small corn cobs sold fresh or canned in brine.

CREAMED available in various sized cans from most supermarkets.

KERNELS sometimes called niblets; available in cans as well as fresh off the cob.

**cornflour** also known as cornstarch; used as a thickening agent in cooking.

**cornmeal** often called polenta, to which this ground dried corn (maize) is similar, albeit coarser. One can be substituted for the other, but textures will vary.

**couscous** a fine, grain-like cereal product, originally from North Africa; made from semolina.

**cream**

FRESH also known as pure cream and pouring cream (minimum fat content 35%); has no additives like commercially thickened cream.

SOUR a thick, commercially cultured, soured cream (minimum fat content 35%); good for dips, toppings and baked cheesecakes.

**cucumber, lebanese** long, slender and thin-skinned; this variety also known as the European or burpless cucumber.

**curry leaves** available fresh or dried and have a mild curry flavour; use like bay leaves.

**eggplant** also known as aubergine.

**eggs** some recipes in this book call for raw or barely cooked eggs; exercise caution if there is a salmonella problem in your area.

**fennel** also known as anise or finocchio; eaten raw in salads or braised or fried as a vegetable accompaniment. Also the name given to dried seeds having a licorice flavour.

**fillo pastry** also known as phyllo; tissue-thin pastry sheets purchased chilled or frozen that are easy to work with and very versatile, lending themselves to both sweet and savoury dishes.

**fish sauce** also called nam pla or nuoc nam; made from pulverised salted fermented fish, most often anchovies. Has a pungent smell and strong taste; use sparingly.

**five-spice powder** a fragrant mixture of ground cinnamon, cloves, star-anise, Sichuan pepper and fennel seeds.

**flour, plain** an all-purpose flour, made from wheat.

**fontina** semi-firm yet creamy, yellow Italian cheese that melts well and has a mild nutty flavour.

**garam masala** a blend of spices, originating in North India; based on varying proportions of cardamom, cinnamon, cloves, coriander, fennel and cumin, roasted and ground together.

**jerusalem artichoke** neither from Jerusalem nor an artichoke; this crunchy tuber tastes a bit like a fresh water chestnut and is related to the sunflower family.

**kalonji** also called black onion seeds or nigella; astringent-tasting seed used in curries and sprinkled on home-made Arab breads such as pide and pitta.

palm sugar

**kaffir lime** wrinkly-skinned, yellow-green fruit and its leaves from a small citrus tree originally grown in South Africa; used in all South-East Asian cuisines.

**kumara** Polynesian name of orange-fleshed sweet potato, often confused with yam.

**lemon grass** a tall, clumping, lemon-smelling and -tasting, sharp-edged grass; the white lower part of each stem is used in Asian cooking.

**mince meat** also known as ground meat.

**noodles**

BEAN-THREAD also called cellophane noodles; made from green mung bean flour.

HOKKIEN also known as stir-fry noodles; fresh egg noodles resembling thick, yellow-brown spaghetti needing no pre-cooking before being used.

**oil**

COOKING-OIL SPRAY vegetable oil in an aerosol can.

OLIVE mono-unsaturated; made from the pressing of tree-ripened olives. "Extra light" or "light" describes the mild flavour, not the fat levels. Extra virgin and virgin

jerusalem artichokes

are the highest quality olive oils, obtained from the first pressings of the olives.

PEANUT pressed from ground peanuts; most commonly used oil in Asian cooking because of its high smoke point.

SESAME made from roasted, crushed, white sesame seeds; a flavouring rather than a cooking medium.

VEGETABLE any of a number of oils sourced from plants rather than animal fats.

**onion**

GREEN also known as scallion or (incorrectly) shallot; an onion picked before the bulb has formed, having a long, bright-green edible stalk.

RED also known as Spanish, red Spanish or Bermuda onion; a sweet-flavoured, large, purple-red onion.

**palm sugar** also known as jaggery, jawa and gula melaka; from the coconut palm. Dark brown to black in colour and usually sold in rock-hard cakes, the sugar of choice in Indian and most of South-East Asian cooking.

**pancetta** an Italian salt-cured pork roll, usually cut from belly pork; used chopped in many dishes to add flavour. Bacon can be substituted.

**parsley, flat-leaf** also known as continental parsley or Italian parsley.

**pide (turkish bread)** comes in long (about 45cm) flat loaves as well as individual rounds; made from wheat flour and sprinkled with sesame or black onion seeds.

**pitta (Lebanese bread)** also spelled pita, this wheat-flour pocket bread is sold in large, flat pieces that separate easily into two thin rounds. Also available in small thick pieces called pocket pitta.

**preserved lemons** a North African specialty recently adopted by cooks all over the world; fruit is preserved in a mixture of salt and lemon juice. Can be rinsed and eaten as is as part of a mezze, or added to casseroles and tagines for their rich salty-sour acidic flavour.

**prosciutto** salt-cured, air-dried (unsmoked), pressed ham; usually sold in paper-thin slices, ready to eat.

**purple shallots** also known as Asian shallots; related to the onion but resembling garlic (they grow in bulbs of multiple cloves). Thin-layered and intensely flavoured, they are used throughout South-East Asia.

**ready-rolled pastry (quiche, puff or shortcrust)** manufactured and sold, under refrigeration or frozen, in sheets or rounds, ready for use with no additional treatment required.

**rice**

ARBORIO small, round-grained white rice, well-suited to absorb a large amount of cooking liquid.

CALROSE medium-size grain; can be used instead of both long- and short-grain varieties.

**risoni** small rice-shape pasta; very similar to another small pasta, orzo.

**rocket** also known as arugula, rugula and rucola; a peppery-tasting green leaf which can be used similarly to baby spinach – eaten raw in salads or cooked in soups, risottos and the like.

**saffron** stigma of a member of the crocus family, available in strands or ground form; imparts a yellow orange colour to food once infused. Quality varies greatly; the best is the most expensive spice in the world. Should be stored in the freezer.

**savoy cabbage** large, heavy head with crinkled dark-green outer leaves; a fairly mild-tasting cabbage.

**sichuan pepper** also known as Chinese pepper; small, red-brown aromatic seeds resembling black peppercorns, they have a peppery-lemon flavour.

**snow peas** also called *mange tout* ("eat all").

**soy sauce** made from fermented soy beans. Several variations are available in most supermarkets and Asian food stores.

**shrimp paste** also known as trasi or blanchan; strong-scented, almost solid preserved paste made of salted dried shrimp. Used for its pungent flavour in many South-East Asian soups and sauces.

**silverbeet** also known as Swiss chard and mistakenly called spinach; a member of the beet family grown for its tasty green leaves and celery-like stems. Best cooked rather than eaten raw.

**spinach** also known as English spinach and, incorrectly, silverbeet. Tender green leaves are good uncooked in salads or added to soups, stir-fries and stews just before serving.

**star-anise** a dried star-shaped pod, the seeds of which have an astringent aniseed flavour.

**tahini** a rich sesame-seed paste, similar to peanut butter in consistency; used in most Middle-Eastern cuisines, particularly Lebanese, in dips and sauces.

**vietnamese mint** not a mint at all, this narrow-leafed, pungent herb, also known as Cambodian mint and laksa leaf (*daun laksa*), is widely used in many Asian soups and salads.

**vinegar**

BALSAMIC authentic only from the province of Modena, Italy; made from a regional wine of white Trebbiano grapes, processed then aged in antique wooden casks.

CIDER made from fermented apple juice.

**wine** the adage is that you should never cook with wine you wouldn't drink; we used good-quality dry white and red wine in our recipes.

**wasabi** an Asian horseradish used to make a fiery sauce traditionally served with Japanese raw fish dishes.

**wonton wrappers** gow gee, egg or spring roll pastry sheets can be substituted.

**zucchini** also known as courgette.

wasabi

# index

# facts and figures

Wherever you live, you'll be able to use our recipes with the help of these easy-to-follow conversions. While these conversions are approximate only, the difference between an exact and the approximate conversion of various liquid and dry measures is but minimal and will not affect your cooking results.

## dry measures

| metric | imperial |
|---|---|
| 15g | 1/2oz |
| 30g | 1oz |
| 60g | 2oz |
| 90g | 3oz |
| 125g | 4oz (1/4lb) |
| 155g | 5oz |
| 185g | 6oz |
| 220g | 7oz |
| 250g | 8oz (1/2lb) |
| 280g | 9oz |
| 315g | 10oz |
| 345g | 11oz |
| 375g | 12oz (3/4lb) |
| 410g | 13oz |
| 440g | 14oz |
| 470g | 15oz |
| 500g | 16oz (1lb) |
| 750g | 24oz (11/2lb) |
| 1kg | 32oz (2lb) |

## liquid measures

| metric | imperial |
|---|---|
| 30ml | 1 fluid oz |
| 60ml | 2 fluid oz |
| 100ml | 3 fluid oz |
| 125ml | 4 fluid oz |
| 150ml | 5 fluid oz (1/4 pint/1 gill) |
| 190ml | 6 fluid oz |
| 250ml | 8 fluid oz |
| 300ml | 10 fluid oz (1/2 pint) |
| 500ml | 16 fluid oz |
| 600ml | 20 fluid oz (1 pint) |
| 1000ml (1 litre) | 13/4 pints |

## helpful measures

| metric | imperial |
|---|---|
| 3mm | 1/8in |
| 6mm | 1/4in |
| 1cm | 1/2in |
| 2cm | 3/4in |
| 2.5cm | 1in |
| 5cm | 2in |
| 6cm | 21/2in |
| 8cm | 3in |
| 10cm | 4in |
| 13cm | 5in |
| 15cm | 6in |
| 18cm | 7in |
| 20cm | 8in |
| 23cm | 9in |
| 25cm | 10in |
| 28cm | 11in |
| 30cm | 12in (1ft) |

## helpful measures

The difference between one country's measuring cups and another's is, at most, within a 2 or 3 teaspoon variance. (For the record, 1 Australian metric measuring cup holds approximately 250ml.) The most accurate way of measuring dry ingredients is to weigh them. When measuring liquids, use a clear glass or plastic jug with the metric markings. (One Australian metric tablespoon holds 20ml; one Australian metric teaspoon holds 5ml.)

If you would like to purchase The Australian Women's Weekly Test Kitchen's metric measuring cups and spoons (as approved by Standards Australia), turn to page 120 for details and an order coupon. You will receive:
- a graduated set of 4 cups for measuring dry ingredients, with sizes marked on the cups.
- a graduated set of 4 spoons for measuring dry and liquid ingredients, with amounts marked on the spoons.

Note: North America, NZ and the UK use 15ml tablespoons. All cup and spoon measurements are level.

We use large eggs having an average weight of 60g.

## oven temperatures

*These oven temperatures are only a guide. Always check the manufacturer's manual.*

| | C° (Celsius) | F° (Fahrenheit) | Gas Mark |
|---|---|---|---|
| Very slow | 120 | 250 | 1 |
| Slow | 150 | 300 | 2 |
| Moderately slow | 160 | 325 | 3 |
| Moderate | 180 - 190 | 350 - 375 | 4 |
| Moderately hot | 200 - 210 | 400 - 425 | 5 |
| Hot | 220 - 230 | 450 - 475 | 6 |
| Very hot | 240 - 250 | 500 - 525 | 7 |

## how to measure

When using graduated metric measuring cups, shake dry ingredients loosely into the appropriate cup. Do not tap the cup on a bench or tightly pack the ingredients unless directed to do so. Level top of measuring cups and measuring spoons with a knife. When measuring liquids, place a clear glass or plastic jug with metric markings on a flat surface to check accuracy at eye level.

# Looking after your interest...

Keep your Home Library cookbooks clean, tidy and within easy reach with slipcovers designed to hold up to 12 books. *Plus* you can follow our recipes perfectly with a set of accurate measuring cups and spoons, as used by *The Australian Women's Weekly* Test Kitchen.

## TO ORDER

**Mail or fax** Photocopy or complete the coupon below and post to AWW Home Library Reader Offer, ACP Direct, PO Box 7036, Sydney NSW 1028, *or* fax to (02) 9267 4363.

**Credit cards** Have your details ready then, if you live in Sydney, phone 9260 0000; if you live elsewhere in Australia, phone 1800 252 515 (free call, Mon-Fri, 8.30am-5.30pm).

## PRICE

**Book Holder** Australia:
pre-GST $11.95, post-GST $13.15
(GST takes effect July 1, 2000).
Elsewhere: $A21.95.

**Metric Measuring Set** Australia:
pre-GST $5.95, post-GST $6.55
(GST takes effect July 1, 2000).
New Zealand: $A8.00.
Elsewhere: $A9.95.
Prices include postage,
handling and GST.
This offer is available
in all countries.

## PAYMENT

**Australian residents** We accept the credit cards listed on the coupon, money orders and cheques.

**Overseas residents** We accept the credit cards listed on the coupon, drafts in $A drawn on an Australian bank, and also British, New Zealand and U.S. cheques in the currency of the country of issue. Credit card charges are at the exchange rate current at the time of payment.

---

✂

☐ **BOOK HOLDER**　　☐ **METRIC MEASURING SET**

*Please indicate number(s) required.*

Mr/Mrs/Ms _____

Address _____

_____

Postcode _____ Country _____

Bus. Hours:( ) _____

y cheque/money order for $_____ payable to ACP Direct

OR: please charge my

☐ Bankcard ☐ Visa ☐ MasterCard ☐ Diners Club ☐ Amex

☐☐☐☐☐☐☐☐☐☐☐☐☐☐☐☐☐☐

Expiry Date ____/____

Cardholder's signature _____

*Please allow up to 30 days for delivery within Australia. Allow up to 6 weeks for overseas deliveries. Both offers expire 30/11/00.*
HLFREEZ00